Rivers of Living Water

Talks on the Holy Spirit

Rivers of Living Water

Talks on the Holy Spirit

Lance Lambert

Richmond, Virginia, USA

ISBN: 978-1-68389-136-9

We have included an exceprt from *The Pilgrim Church* by E.H. Broadbent. Public domain. See beginning on page 166.

Cover art by: Angelina Guhl
www.lancelambert.org

Contents

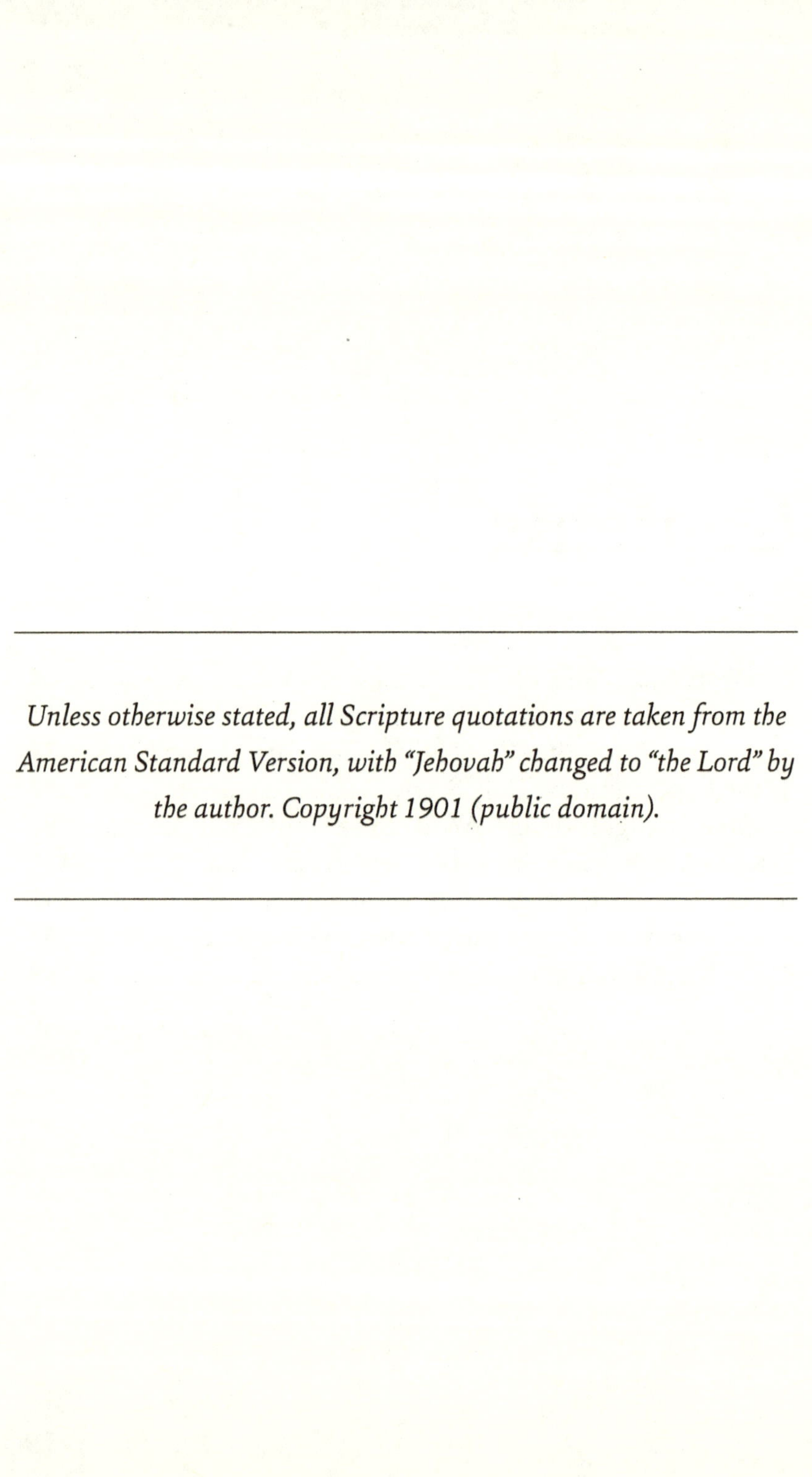

Foreword

This book is a compilation of messages Lance spoke on the Holy Spirit over many years. Typically, we prefer to publish his series of ministries to ensure the cohesive reading experience Lance intended. It seems, however, the Holy Spirit has led to compile these as a collection.

Several of these messages came to our attention and, around the same time, a brother called and testified to how Lance's sharing on the baptism of the Holy Spirit, along with several others, were used in a wonderful way for him and several young people as a result. He felt that these would benefit the body of Christ in our day and a book may be of help. The very same day a sister brought these back up to consider releasing these same messages on our podcast (which are now available).

Grateful to do so, we began to prepare these for print. These need not be read consecutively as they were delivered at various times and locations throughout Lance's ministry. However, we have given an attempt to place them in an order that may be of help to the reader who may read them from cover to cover. There is overlapping and similar content in a few chapters. Yet Lance highlighted different aspects in each of these chapters which make each one a worthy read, giving a unique view of the person of the Holy Spirit.

We have been blessed by the help of many on this collection, and we would love to give special thanks to a dear sister for her labour of love. She, in the city of Jerusalem, which is still often having to take refuge in the midst of missiles, has continued faithfully reviewing these messages. She has been a blessing to this ministry for many years, as well as faithful in the various ways the Lord has called her to serve. We pray for her and those in Israel that the Lord's prayer on their behalf would be answered.

We cannot confidently identify the dates or locations Lance delivered most of these ministries. If these details are of help to you, we encourage you to notice details mentioned in the text. For instance, a pope's visit to Poland, which was likely in 1979. Or "the brink of this week of prayer" as likely being spoken at a prayer conference.

Lastly, the chapter on "The Manifestation of the Holy Spirit" has been added as an encouragement with many testimonies of the work of the Holy Spirit. This chapter is also included in Lance's title *My House Shall Be a House of Prayer* yet we felt this would be a great encouragement in light of the other messages contained in this collection.

May the Lord meet you with His presence and a revealing of who this third person of the trinity is to us as you seek Him with us for all He longs you to know of Himself. "Faithful is He that calleth you, who will also do it."

1.
Christ as Baptiser in the Holy Spirit

Matthew 3:11–12
I indeed baptize you in water unto repentance: but he that cometh after me is mightier than I, whose shoes I am not worthy to bear: he shall baptize you in the Holy Spirit and in fire: whose fan is in his hand, and he will thoroughly cleanse his threshing-floor; and he will gather his wheat into the garner, but the chaff he will burn up with unquenchable fire.

Mark 1:7–8
And he preached, saying, There cometh after me he that is mightier than I, the latchet of whose shoes I am not worthy to stoop down and unloose. I baptized you in water; but he shall baptize you in the Holy Spirit.

Luke 3:15–17
And as the people were in expectation, and all men reasoned in their hearts concerning John, whether haply he were the Christ; John answered, saying unto them all, I indeed baptize you with water; but there cometh he that is mightier than I, the latchet of

whose shoes I am not worthy to unloose: he shall baptize you in the Holy Spirit and in fire: whose fan is in his hand, thoroughly to cleanse his threshing-floor, and to gather the wheat into his garner; but the chaff he will burn up with unquenchable fire.

John 1:29–34

On the morrow he seeth Jesus coming unto him, and saith, Behold, the Lamb of God, that taketh away the sin of the world! This is he of whom I said, After me cometh a man who is become before me: for he was before me. And I knew him not; but that he should be made manifest to Israel, for this cause came I baptizing in water. And John bare witness, saying, I have beheld the Spirit descending as a dove out of heaven; and it abode upon him. And I knew him not: but he that sent me to baptize in water, he said unto me, Upon whomsoever thou shalt see the Spirit descending, and abiding upon him, the same is he that baptizeth in the Holy Spirit. And I have seen, and have borne witness that this is the Son of God.

Acts 1:4–5

And, being assembled together with them, he charged them not to depart from Jerusalem, but to wait for the promise of the Father, which, said he, ye heard from me: for John indeed baptized with water; but ye shall be baptized in the Holy Spirit not many days hence.

Shall we just bow together in a word of prayer?

Heavenly Father, we just want to bow here in Your presence and we want very simply to recognise that apart from You, we can do nothing. Whether it is in speaking or hearing, Lord, we can do nothing. We can speak words. We can hear words. But, Lord, if something of Your purpose for this time is to be fulfilled, then You need to be here Yourself and You need by Your Spirit to reveal things and illuminate things and so anoint, Lord, both speaking and hearing, that Your glorious purpose, Your specific purpose for a time such as this, be fulfilled. Then, Lord, we commit ourselves to You by faith, taking that anointing which is ours for the speaker and for every hearer. In the name of our Lord Jesus. Amen.

The burden I have had has been centred in these words in II Corinthians 11:2–3:

> *For I am jealous over you with a godly jealousy: for I espoused you to one husband, that I might present you as a pure virgin to Christ. But I fear, lest by any means, as the serpent beguiled Eve in his craftiness, your minds should be corrupted from the simplicity and the purity that is toward Christ.*

In these last days, in this last phase of world history, you and I need to get clear that the end of our walk with the Lord, of all the dealings of the Lord with us, of all Christian life, of all service and work and of church life, is that you and I should be presented a pure virgin to Christ, that we should not have our minds corrupted from the singleness which is toward Him, the unaffectedness which is toward Him, that our mind should not be corrupted from the purity which is toward Him.

We consider the need of knowing the Lord Jesus as our covering.

That is foundational, not kindergarten. It is foundational. If you and I have not had revealed to us something of the nature of the atoning work of the Lord Jesus, something of the nature of justification, something of what it means for Him who knew no sin to be made sin for us, that we might become the righteousness of God in Him, we shall be compromised, contaminated, diverted, tripped up by the enemy somewhere along the way, and certainly in these last days. For this accuser of the brethren will have come down onto the earth, knowing his time is short, and will do such an insidious and such a powerful work that there will not be two brothers left together. There will not be a fellowship in harmony with each other in the Lord. There will not be even peace between believers and their Lord. We need to know the Lord Jesus as our covering. "They overcame the accuser of the brethren by the blood of the Lamb."

Christ Our Life and Our Power

Now, I would like to share about Christ as our life and our power, and I find it a tremendous joy and a tremendous discovery to find that the Lord Jesus is the life. There is no such thing as the Christian life. You know, this Christian life is so complex. I do not know if you have discovered that yet, but it is the most complex thing in the whole world. Trying to be holy in an unholy world is a dreadful business. Trying to turn the other cheek in a world that's continually hitting you is no easy matter.

It's bad enough amongst the believers when they are hitting you. You must have all discovered that. We talk so much about the Christian life. The interesting thing is the Christian life is not mentioned once in the whole Bible. You would almost think it does not exist. But what we call the Christian life, the New Testament calls eternal life, that is, the life of Jesus. That life of Jesus is communicated to us, transmitted to us in the person of the Holy Spirit.

You don't have to try and tie apples on an apple tree to make it fruitful. If you do, it may look pretty, but it's a dreadful job. Can you imagine going down to the supermarket, buying so many pounds of apples, then going out to the poor old tree, getting a ladder, going up in it, and tying each apple on the branches? Now, my dear friends, for a few days it will look good, which is what happens with many people in these kinds of conferences. The apples are tied on the branches; they look pretty good. But within a week, the apples have withered. They never came out of the life in the apple tree. They never went through the organic process. They do not actually belong to that particular apple tree. They have been borrowed from another. That is what it means to be affected. That is why we need this simplicity of Christ to get back to the simple truth that Jesus is the life.

If you and I would only see that Jesus is the life—that He dwells within us and is free to work in us—and if we will obey the law of the life, then we will have fruit. There will be fruit, there will be character, there will be fulfilment.

Our problem is getting the life flowing. There is no way to know the release of the life of the Lord Jesus in a human being apart from the work of the cross. In other words, you must know death so that His life may flow through you. That is our problem. The thought of dying, somehow for many of us, is not part of the gospel. That He should die for us, that is the gospel, but that we should die with Him, that is not the gospel.

We are here to get what we can. Life, salvation, an eternal position in the kingdom of God, peace, joy, power, anything—but we do not want to die. Now when we cannot come to that simple falling into the ground and dying, we may know all the theory, but the life of Jesus is trapped within you. It will never be expressed, it will never grow, it will never bear fruit. It is trapped within you, it is there, but it is trapped within you.

Or again, think of Jesus as the power. What a need there is for power! For example, the power to pray. Some people are so frightened, they cannot even open their mouths in a time of prayer and when they do, you cannot hear them. They are so afraid. No power.

When you've got no power, you become self-conscious. All you are conscious of is your inadequacy, your inability, your unworthiness, everything that you are. But when there is power, you can forget yourself and get on with the job.

You can minister to the Lord. You can minister to your brothers and sisters. You can witness spontaneously, not in that dreadful cornering of some poor soul and asking them if they have seen the light or whether they are saved. What a disaster this has been. God used D.L. Moody so greatly in this way, but many believers that have followed have not been so singularly blessed in following the technique of D.L. Moody. People corner unbelievers, shove a tract in their hand, tell them that they are going to hell, that they need the Lord.

That is not what I mean by witnessing. I mean that when people begin to note that there is a fire in you and there is a life in you, and there is a love in you, and there is a peace in you, and there is a joy in you, they begin to ask about this, and then you have an answer. You are able to share the Lord Jesus in the most spontaneous, unaffected, normal way.

Such power. Jesus is the power. It is the power of His resurrection. Doesn't that give the clue straight away that if we are to know the power of His resurrection, we have to know something of what it is to die with Him? In other words, there is no power unless you and I are broken, unless you and I become weak, then the power of the Lord Jesus tabernacles upon us.

But that is not my subject at this time, though I would like to talk very much about it. But to know Christ as the life and the power, that is tremendous. What I want to talk about this morning is to know Christ as the baptiser in the Spirit.

Christ as Our Baptiser

Now, I am very well aware that this is the most controversial subject, but I have to point out to you that at the beginning of all four Gospels and the beginning of the book of Acts, we have this phrase, "He shall baptise you in the Holy Spirit and fire."

You cannot get away from it. It must be not only vitally important, but deeply significant.

It is not as if one of the Gospels mentions it and none of the others do. Every one of the four Gospels, the three synoptic Gospels and John, which is the interpretation, every one of them mentions this statement of John the Baptist, "I indeed baptise you in water, but He that cometh after Me, He shall baptise you in the Holy Spirit and in fire."

So, when we come to the book of the Acts, which is another foundational book as far as the gospel goes, we discover right at the beginning the words of the Lord Jesus, "John indeed baptised you with water, but you shall be baptised in the Holy Spirit not many days hence" (Acts 1:5).

Now I want just to point out two or three things. I know that there is colossal controversy over this subject, and I know that it would be much easier not to use the word baptism of the Spirit. In this way we worm out of it and everybody is happy. But the fact is, the Book speaks of this *baptism in the Spirit*, and therefore it is best for us to face squarely what it's all about.

John's Baptism Preparing the Way

Now, it is interesting how John the Baptist described the heart of his ministry. I do not suppose there is a single one of us who has any question about the calling of John the Baptist. We know that he was called by God. He was a man sent by God. He was a fulfilment of Isaiah's prophetic word, a voice crying in the wilderness, "Make ready, make straight a way for the Lord."

This John the Baptist described his ministry as, "I indeed baptise you in water," as if that was the summing up of his ministry, his call to repentance, his call to turn away from an old life, from an old way. As if in this baptism it was a preparation for the coming kingdom. He summed it up in his baptism. When certain people tried to misuse and abuse his ministry, certain Sadducees and Pharisees, he said to them, "Who warned you, you brood of vipers, to escape from the wrath that is coming?" It wasn't just a little ritual that he didn't mind administering to anybody and everybody. John, as far as was in him, wanted to be certain that everyone who was baptised understood a little at least of what they were doing.

Now, he described and summed up his ministry, the heart of it, as this baptism in water. If you had lived in those days, then you would have been identified with the purpose of God at that particular time in history by being baptised with John's baptism. That is how you would have identified yourself with the purpose of God, with the phase of the purpose of God that the people of God were in.

This John the Baptist describes the heart of the Messiah's ministry as "He shall baptise you in the Holy Spirit and in fire."

Now I just find it impossible to relegate that to some sort of shelf, theologically, and say, "Oh, well, don't put too much on that. There are much more important things than that. If you'd be rolling on the floor and sort of behaving in an inordinate manner, all that kind of thing, if that's what you're talking about, I mean ... I'm not going to alienate myself from believers who've had such an exotic experience. But I don't catch the heart of things."

But what an extraordinary thing if John the Baptist were to describe the heart of his ministry as baptism in water, and the heart of the Lord Jesus' ministry as baptism in the Spirit and in fire, and it is only an exotic experience for elite people, something that is not necessary, that is only for a few, perhaps one segment of the family of God. I do not believe we can ignore or devalue this whole matter without doing serious damage to our own life in the Lord and to the service of God that we are involved in and in the church life that you and I long to see.

The Holy Spirit Prepares the Way

Now, I say there is colossal controversy over this matter, but I think we can clear the ground of certain misapprehensions. First of all, there is nothing at all possible without the person of the Holy Spirit. For instance, there is no such thing as repentance and conviction of sin without the person of the Holy Spirit. If you look in John 16:7–8, Jesus said:

> *Nevertheless I tell you the truth: It is expedient for you that I go away; for if I go not away, the Comforter will not come unto you; but if I go, I will send Him unto you. And He, when He is come, will convict the world in respect of sin, and of righteousness, and of judgment.*

In other words, there is not a single person who has repented from their sin, who has been convicted of their lost state, who has been convicted of their destiny for hell, but by the Holy Spirit. Nor has there ever been a single believer who has become convinced that Jesus is the Messiah, the Son of the living God, apart from the work of the Holy Spirit. They may not know it. They may never have heard of the Holy Spirit. But it is the Holy Spirit who takes the salvation of the Lord Jesus, who is at the right hand of God the Father, and makes it a living reality to a human being.

Who opened your eyes? Who caused you first to behold the Lamb of God who taketh away the sin of the world? The person of the Holy Spirit. You did not even know Him, but it was He who graciously came to you and began to lead you, pricking your conscience with a conviction of sin and a knowing of righteousness and of judgment, and leading you into a vision, however dim, of the Lord Jesus as the Lamb of God, the Saviour of the world.

Born Again by the Spirit

No one can be born again of God apart from the Holy Spirit. Jesus said, "You must be born of water and of the Spirit" (John 3:5). There is no way that anyone can be born again unto a living hope through the resurrection of Jesus Christ from the dead, apart from the person of the Holy Spirit. How else?

There is no way. You may not even have known it, but you are born of God. You are in the family of God. The Spirit of God has been shed abroad in your heart, crying, "Abba Father!" For the first time you have a relationship with God. He is Father to you, not just some awesome God. He is Father.

Life and Power by the Spirit

Or again, there can be no life and power without the Holy Spirit. In Romans 8:6 it says:

> *For the mind of the flesh is death; but the mind of the Spirit is life and peace.*

Or again, I think of those words in Acts 1:8:

> *Ye shall receive power, when the Holy Spirit is come upon you: and ye shall be My witnesses ...*

There is no other way that you can know the life of the Lord Jesus without the Holy Spirit. The Lord Jesus, if I may put it very poorly and almost irreverently, is the located person of the Godhead.

Do you understand what I am trying to say? What I am saying is this, that the Lord Jesus is at the right hand of God the Father. How then are you in Christ? How then can you know the resurrection life of Christ? Only by the Spirit. There is no other way. For the Holy Spirit is everywhere at one time. He has no body. Do you understand what I mean?

Now, I am very well aware that whenever we touch the Trinity, we are touching essential mystery. I am not at all sure that any one of us, I in particular, would ever be able to interpret or adequately explain the Godhead. But what I do know is this: nowhere in the New Testament does it say that Jesus is everywhere. He is at the right hand of the majesty on high from whence He shall come. As God, He is everywhere, but He even bears in His hands and His side and His feet the marks of His passion. The God-man, the Word made flesh who dwelt among us.

But the Spirit of the Lord, He is everywhere, and He makes the Lord Jesus at the right hand of the majesty on high, a living reality in any human being. He transmits the power of the Lord Jesus. He is the one who opens the eyes of those who are fatherless to the fullness of the Lord Jesus. He is the one who leads us into everything that the Lord Jesus is. The Spirit of truth who leads us into all truth. Or I like it another way, the Spirit of reality who leads us into all reality.

There can be no fruit without the person of the Holy Spirit. For it says in Galatians 5:22, "the fruit of the Spirit." There can be no fruit without the Spirit. That is why so many Christian lives are religious. They are not spiritual. They are not living the Christ life. They are religious lives. They are saved, but there is no organic fruit being produced by the indwelling Christ through the person of the Holy Spirit.

I hope I am getting this over to you. For the Holy Spirit is the ignored person of the Trinity. For many, He is an "it," an influence, a power, an agency, instead of God the Spirit.

The Holy Spirit and the Cross

You know, the discovery of the person of the Holy Spirit is as tremendous as a discovery of the person of Christ. Now, my dear friends, let me just go on and get this right over to you. There is no such thing as any experience of the cross apart from the Holy Spirit. Oh, would to God this could burn into every heart. I have been in so many places, especially in Europe, where I have seen people who have got this teaching of the cross, and they are bound, crabby, narrow, strait-laced, without any life or power at all! Yet they have got the whole teaching of the cross up here in their heads!

My dear friends, you can apprehend the teaching of the cross mentally! You can make it an affliction of the flesh. You can make it a will worship. "I'm going to suffer. I am going to suffer!" My dear friend, if you have ever suffered or know anything of the fellowship of the sufferings of the Lord, you will never again say, "I am going to suffer." It is something inescapable, but you will not ask for it. You know that it is something that lies in the way, "through many tribulations, we enter into the kingdom of God."

Now, my dear friends, we can make this whole matter of the

cross a heaviness, a darkness, a sombreness, a seriousness which is religion! This is what the Hindus do. Even the Buddhists are a bit more light-headed. It is a matter of religion.

I think of those poor saints—I do not want to be disrespectful, I may have to meet some of them one day—but when I think of some of those poor saints in the early ages of the church who sat up on poles in the desert—well, they had to be Greek. That is not meant to be anything unkind to anybody here who is Greek. But it is a mentality that you must do affliction to the body in order to save the spirit! They sat up on top of poles all day and all night and had the food put up on another pole—very little of it, of course. I have sometimes walked in the wadis and valleys around Jerusalem and the wilderness of Judea and there, to this day, you can see some of the caves that are walled up. There are still some who have never been out of those walled up caves. A little bit of food is put through a little hole to them. They spend their lives, they say, in prayer and devotion. Now, God forbid that I should devalue them if it really is of God, but I can only say the Lamas do it in Tibet.

We can make this matter of the cross just something like that, but the Book says, "If by the Spirit you do put to death the deeds of the body, ye shall live." The whole work of the cross is not simply to leave us in some kind of sombre sobriety, a kind of heavy bondage. The whole work of the cross is to move us into resurrection, into fruit, into life, into power, something swallowed up by the Lord.

The real work of the cross is impossible without the Holy Spirit, and I have noticed that in those who really have an experience of the cross—thank God there are many who really have such a real experience—you see the beauty of the Lord upon their very faces.

You see a radiance shining out of their inner man. You see when you touch them, something of the Lord Jesus. There is a fragrance left by their presence.

The Holy Spirit and Church Life

Well, take church life. There can be no true church life without the person of the Holy Spirit. Without His leading all it is, is a collection of people with an understanding of the nature of the church, as denominational as anything else, because they make the very truth of the church a thing and they divide from others so that it becomes, in the end, just like everything else. "They are built on baptism, someone else is built on tongues, somebody else is built on a second experience of sanctification, somebody else is built on gifts or something, and we are built on the truth of the church." But that is not the church. The church is inclusive. Everyone born of God is in the church. We belong to them and they to us. We are not partakers of other men's sins, but, my dear friends, all the difference between an inclusive spirit and an exclusive spirit is when the Holy Spirit begins to bring believers together and relate them one to another, so that they begin to flow together, so that they begin to maintain the unity of the Spirit together, so that they begin to function by the power of the Holy Spirit, then the church is built and the testimony of Jesus is held. Otherwise, we are forever talking about truth and never experiencing church life in reality. Oh, we need the Holy Spirit.

I do not think I need to say that gifts and equipment for service are impossible without the Holy Spirit. There are some strange notions. I was once standing in a queue for lunch and this is where, generally speaking, most people get hold of me for theological questions (either then or when we are eating). This brother said to me, "Oh, brother," putting his arm on my back, "Isn't it wonderful to know Jesus?" "Oh," I said, "yes, it is!" He was a dear old brother. Then he said to me, "What do you think about the gifts of the Holy Spirit?" So, trying to think of my meal, I looked at him straight in the eyes and said, "I believe there are such things as gifts of the Spirit."

"Brother," he said, "Jesus is enough for me!"

"Oh," I said, "well, He's enough for me. But, evidently, I don't see it as you do. You see the gifts of the Spirit there and Jesus here. I see the gifts of the Spirit as gifts of Jesus. Every time there is a real gift of the Spirit manifested, there's something more of Jesus deposited because it is Jesus who is being manifested."

He looked at me in a rather sad manner, and then I said to him, "Do you mean to tell me if you had appendicitis and you had to be rushed into the hospital, and operated on, and your wife came to you and said, 'Don't worry, dear. The man who's going to operate on you has degrees like this behind his name.' But when he came, he came with a tree saw, a chisel, a hacksaw and some garden shoes." I said, "Would you be happy? You think, 'It doesn't matter. This man has character. This man has maturity. That's all that matters.' My dear friend," I said, "I think if your appendix were coming out, you'd like him to have character, maturity *and* the right equipment."

How can you and I do the job that God has given us to do if we do not have the right gifts and the right equipment? It is a monstrous idea. It is an error. You and I need the gifts and the equipment of the Holy Spirit, and we can only have them with the Holy Spirit. Any gift or any equipment that is not through the work and person of the Holy Spirit is counterfeit and dangerous.

The Holy Spirit and the Lordship of Jesus Christ

Nobody can call Jesus "Lord" except by the Holy Spirit. That is what it says in 1 Corinthians 12:3:

> *No man can say, Jesus is Lord, but by the Holy Spirit.*

Now, my dear friends, in the Greek, it is very interesting. This is how it puts it. "No man can say Jesus is Lord except *in* the Holy Spirit."

Try.

I know that those who are really afflicted by the enemy are not even able to call Jesus Lord. I know that. But I am not meaning only things that perhaps are a little more superficial. Have you ever found a single believer or a single company of believers that is really under the Lordship of Jesus, hearing the will of God, hearing the word of God, and obeying? Except in the Holy Spirit, there is no way to do it. Everybody puts their own little heads together and either with a consensus of opinion or from one man's opinion, they do what they think is right.

They say, "Jesus is Lord!" He is not Lord. People go off and say the Lord has told them to do something and He has not had anything to do with it at all. They just want to do their own thing. When later they discover it is wrong, they say, "Oh, the Lord has shown me something else." As if the Lord does not know His own mind! First, He takes them here, then there, then back, then forward, then over here, then back. It is ridiculous, but they say it is all "the Lord."

It makes a mockery of the lordship of Jesus. There is no way to know the lordship of Jesus until you are in the Holy Spirit, your spiritual ear has been opened to hear the voice of God.

My dear friends, you see, I think this is quite an important matter. I do not know why people are so afraid of the Holy Spirit. What is there to be afraid of in the Holy Spirit?

I have in my little life found the Holy Spirit to be two things to me at one and the same time. He is the most gentle, the most sweet and the most marvellous person in handling me. At the same time, He is the most firm, (if I may put it in one way) the most obstinate, the most uncompromising person in dealing with me. There is nothing to be afraid of as far as the Holy Spirit is concerned. He has come to take you home. Yet if you are going to have problems with Him all the way through, you are going to make it very difficult.

He wants to change you from sinner to saint (and that is a job!). He wants to conform you to the image of the Lord Jesus. Oh, the glory of it! The ugliest of us. There are plenty of us whom He wants to take—those who are by nature so difficult, so ugly, so unlike Christ, and conform us to the image of God's Son. What in the world is wrong with us that we are so afraid of the Holy Spirit?

I hope this does not upset anybody, but I do not mean it in the malicious way. But you know, you can talk about Jesus as a form of escapism. You can almost talk about Jesus and everything being in Jesus and Jesus being everything. Yet in reality you do not know the life and nature and power of Jesus because you are avoiding the person of the Holy Spirit.

Only the Holy Spirit can make the life and nature and power of Jesus a living reality, both in me and in you and in us as the church.

Immersed

Would you note something about this statement we find in all four of the Gospels?

He that baptiseth in the Holy Spirit and fire.

Now, I do not know about you. I do not know your theological persuasion. I think I know quite a lot here, but I understand baptism as immersion. I do not think anybody with a Jewish background could understand baptism in any other way, because that's the way everybody was baptised in the time of Jesus. Before the Christian baptism, not even just considering John's baptism (what we call proselyte baptism), we have found through Jerusalem in every single one of the Jewish sites uncovered in the whole of the Middle East, baptistry after baptistry after baptistry, after baptistry. We now see that everybody was immersed. Everybody tried to keep the truth away for religious reasons, but now we know.

The very word in Greek means *to dip*. Originally, primitively, it means *to dip*. In fact, it is used in classical Greek of dyeing a garment. Now, have you ever heard of someone taking a garment and you want to change it from yellow to deep green and you sprinkle green dye over it?! Nobody has ever heard of such a thing. Or suppose you take a piece of yellow cloth and you say,

"Well, I won't sprinkle, but I will pour some dye over it." You are going to have a very blotchy business. What do you do when you dye material? You dip the whole thing in a great vat of dye, and it goes completely in and out! You do not leave it in. Who can wear a piece of cloth that is left in the dye? You have got to get it out. Something goes in and comes out. That is baptism. You go into the waters and you come out of the waters. In the waters you are immersed. You are "dyed."

Now listen again. "He that cometh after me, He shall immerse you in the Holy Spirit." For me, this takes this whole question out of controversy and puts it into a new dimension. Immersed in the person of the Holy Spirit! My dear friends, sometimes I hear people have had an experience of the Holy Spirit and I would have imagined from the way they have talked that they have "got" the Holy Spirit. It is as if they have somehow obtained the Spirit, trapped the Spirit, encompassed the Spirit. They have got the Spirit located. They have got Him.

I do not find this to be baptism in the Spirit. I find this baptism is that you are dipped in the Holy Spirit. You are immersed in the Holy Spirit. Somehow or other you discover that it is not that you got the Spirit, the Holy Spirit has got you.

Do you notice that John the Baptist does not say, "He shall baptise you in spirit and fire?" He does not say that. He says very carefully in every instance in the Gospels, "He shall baptise you in the Holy Spirit and in fire."

In other words, this marvellous thought is that you and I should somehow or other be immersed in the person of the Holy Spirit. I think of these words of Jesus that come to me in John 7:37–39:

Now on the last day, the great day of the feast, Jesus stood and cried, saying, If any man thirst, let him come unto Me and drink. He that believeth on Me, as the scripture hath said, from within him shall flow rivers of living water. But this spake He of the Spirit, which they that believed on Him were to receive: for the Spirit was not yet given; because Jesus was not yet glorified.

"If any man thirst, let him come unto Me and drink." That is how we get born of God, isn't it? We receive the Spirit then and He comes to live within us. But then there is something else. "He that believeth on Me, as the scripture says, from within him shall flow out rivers of living water"! Not a stream—rivers of living water, able to turn desert areas into a garden, able to transform whole great areas around us. *Rivers of living water.*

Dear, dear friend, note it is all to do with Jesus. "He that believeth." not on the Spirit, but, "He that believeth on Me, from within him shall flow out rivers of living water." I believe that it is almost every time you believe more deeply in the Lord Jesus, the rivers of God flow out of you in a fuller way. It is a faith position.

Or I think of the wonderful words in Colossians 2:9–10, I expect all of you know them so well. "For in Him," that is in Christ, "dwelleth all the fullness of the Godhead bodily. And in Him ye are made full,"—in Him—not He in you, trapped inside of you, but in Him you are made full, as if your little vessel is submerged in the fullness of God in Christ.

Or again I think of another marvellous word. I am sure these are so well known to you. In Ephesians 3:16–19, listen to these words:

That He would grant you, according to the riches of His glory, that ye may be strengthened with power through His Spirit in the inward man; that Christ may dwell in your hearts through faith; to the end that ye, being rooted and grounded in love, may be strong to apprehend with all the saints what is the breadth and length and height and depth, and to know the love of Christ which passeth knowledge, that ye may be filled unto all the fullness of God.

Theory, theology, ideal or reality? For many believers, it is an ideal.

It is meant to be a reality. For on the day of Pentecost, when the Lord Jesus obtained the promise of the Spirit and poured Him forth, then it was as if those 120 suddenly were submerged in a fullness they had never known before. Rivers of living water began to flow out of them, to turn the whole Roman world and far beyond it upside down, to turn a wilderness into a garden.

They were filled to all the fullness of God, so filled that people looking at them thought they were drunk. Something had taken them over, submerged them as it were—overflowed. Would to God the meetings of our fellowships and assemblies were like that, overflowing with the Lord.

Oh, my dear friends, I think of a little poem by Amy Carmichael. It is one that has meant a lot to me:

Upon the sandy shore an empty shell,
Beyond the shell infinity of sea;
O Saviour, I am like that empty shell;
Thou art the sea to me.

A sweeping wave rides up the shore and lo,
Each dim recess the coiled shell within
Is searched, is filled, is filled to overflow
By water crystalline.

Not to the shell is any glory then:
All glory give we to the glorious sea.
And not to me is any glory when
Thou overflowest me.

Sweep over me, Thy shell, as low I lie,
I yield me to the purposes of Thy will;
Sweep up, O conquering waves, and purify.
And with Thy fulness fill.

That is what it means to be immersed in the Holy Spirit.

Fire

But there is something else that cannot go from it until we have just said it. It is fire!

Now, I think fire is the most wonderful thing in the whole world, really, and also the most terrible thing. Fire speaks of warmth, of love. It speaks of energy and power. It speaks of radiance and light. It speaks of refining and purity. The symbol of the new covenant is fire. On the day of Pentecost, it was a rushing sound of a mighty wind that came in and fire fell upon every one of them.

Fire has caught those who had a gift for poetry or hymn

writing. I think of Charles Wesley's wonderful hymn. I wish we had it to sing:

O Thou who camest from above,
the pure celestial fire to impart
kindle a flame of sacred love
upon the mean altar of my heart.

There let it for Thy glory burn
with inextinguishable blaze,
and trembling to its source return,
in humble prayer and fervent praise.

Jesus, confirm my heart's desire
to work and speak and think for Thee;
still let me guard the holy fire,
and still stir up Thy gift in me.

Ready for all Thy perfect will,
my acts of faith and love repeat,
till death Thy endless mercies seal,
and make the sacrifice complete.

No wonder God owned men like that. Or I think again of another little word by Amy Carmichael. I do not know if it means anything to you:

But I have seen a fiery flame
Take to His pure and burning heart

Mere dust of earth, to it impart
His virtue, till that dust became
Transparent loveliness of flame.

O Fire of God, Thou fervent Flame,
Thy dust of earth in Thee would fall,
And so be lost beyond recall,
Transformed by Thee, its very name
Forgotten in Thine own, O Flame.

My dear friends, that is fire.

If that does not awaken in you a hunger, nothing will. You will never win another soul to Christ if there is not fire in you. No one will ever turn aside to see this great sight, unless you are a thorn bush burning with fire and not being consumed.

It is fire. Oh, my dear friends, I think of Moses' cry when he had seen so much and heard so much, "Show me Thy glory."

The Baptiser

So, my friends, here's the last point: I want you to note that the whole emphasis in all four Gospels in this statement is not, if I may say it reverently, on the person of the Holy Spirit as much as the baptiser.

"He shall baptise you in the Holy Spirit and in fire." There is only one person in the universe who can take you, saved by the grace of God, and immerse you in the person of the Holy Spirit and in fire, and that is the Lord Jesus. He is the baptiser. Your zeal will not bring it about. Your waiting will not bring it about. Your tears will not bring it about. Your sacrifice will not bring it about. Your knowledge will not bring it about. Your devotion will not bring it about. Not even your good works can bring upon you that immersion in the person of the Holy Spirit. There is only one who can do it. He is the one who died for you. Because He died for you, He has won for you an eternal and so great salvation, He has won for you a birthright. The birthright is for you to be immersed in the person of the Holy Spirit.

When we see Jesus at the right hand of God the Father and we see that He has obtained the promise of the Father and poured forth this which we see and hear, then for the first time, we might understand He is the one who can take you and me and immerse us in the person of the Holy Spirit and in fire.

Dear friends, there will be no way in which you and I will be presented a pure virgin to the Lord Jesus apart from the person of the Holy Spirit.

I do not know about you, I don't know whether your circumstances are too much for you. I will tell you; no amount of knowledge will get you over those circumstances. You can know all mysteries and all kinds of things. It may help you quite considerably. But you will not come through those circumstances unscathed.

Perhaps you have got situations too much for you and you say, "Well, if I'm more devoted, won't it help?" Of course it will, but it will not change the situation. The only way that you and I can come through these things is by being immersed in the person of the Holy Spirit. It is like the tide coming up and covering everything.

Oh, dear brother and sister, may God open your eyes and

deliver you from this spirit of controversy over this subject. Over different techniques, different steps, different ways. I am not bothered about that. All I am bothered about is this: Do you know Jesus as the baptiser in the Holy Spirit and in fire?

You say, "Well, yes, I'm converted." I did not ask that. I know you are converted. I know you are saved.

Well, you say, "I'm walking with Lord."

Yes, yet, I am asking whether you are immersed in the person of the Holy Spirit and in fire.

If God were to open our eyes to see Jesus as the one whose finished work has obtained the promise of the Father and poured forth the Holy Spirit, then you and I may come to know what it is to be lost in the fullness and power of God. May the Lord do it for every one of us in these last days and may that glorious power and fire of the Holy Spirit enable us to be unaffected, single-hearted and single-eyed, not corrupted from the simplicity and purity which is toward Christ.

2.
The True Anointing—The Holy Spirit's Part in Our Lives

Psalm 133

Behold how good and how pleasant it is for brethren to dwell together in unity. It is like the precious oil upon the head that ran down upon the beard, even Aaron's beard that came down upon the skirt of his garments, like the dew of Hermon that cometh down upon the mountains of Zion. For there the Lord commanded the blessing, even life forevermore.

This is a very short psalm, but it contains everything. Now, we are going to go for a little wander in the word together. But we're going to start here in Psalm 133. I'm going to talk about the true anointing, and I want you to notice straightaway, in verse two, that we've got the principle picture in the Old Testament of anointing. "It is like the precious oil upon the head that ran down upon the beard, even Aaron's beard that came down upon the skirt of his garments." That is what the psalm is all about. It is about an anointing.

Everything else in this little psalm comes out of the anointing. This is true in the Christian life as well, for the anointing oil speaks of the Holy Spirit. I think most people know that oil in Scripture (particularly the anointing oil) is a symbol or a type of the Holy Spirit.

This anointing oil, as we shall see later on, was a special mixture. You were not allowed—it was, in fact, a criminal offence—to use it for anything else other than the service of God and according to the mind of God. It was holy, separated unto the Lord.

I think most of you know the high priest was anointed, the priests were anointed, the kings were anointed, the prophets were anointed; it was a picture of entering into service by the appointment and the enabling power of God. In other words, not only was this an authoritative declaration that God was setting aside this person for service, but it was also the wherewithal to serve the Lord. In other words, within the very anointing was the actual ability to serve the Lord. I think that is very important for us to understand. So, that is the first thing about this Psalm 133. We have got something about precious oil.

The Preciousness of the Holy Spirit

Now, I don't think there is anything in the whole of life more precious than the ministry of the Holy Spirit. For without that exceedingly precious ministry, that vital ministry of the Holy Spirit, there could be absolutely nothing at all for any of us. It is He who moved upon the face of the waters and brought order out of chaos, substance out of emptiness, light out of darkness. It was by Him that God's purpose was, as it were, watched over through the years. It was by Him that the Lord Jesus was born of the virgin Mary. It was the Holy Spirit who anointed the Lord Jesus, when Jesus was 30 years of age, in the waters of the Jordan after He came up from His baptism.

Well, we can go on and on. It was the Holy Spirit who enabled the Lord Jesus to offer Himself up on the cross and it was the Holy Spirit that raised Jesus from the dead; that lifeless body was raised from the dead. You all know about Pentecost, when the risen Christ ascended into glory and took His position at the right hand of God the Father, then the Holy Spirit was released in an altogether new way. He had always been present. He had always been ministering. But Pentecost marked an absolutely new giving of the Holy Spirit to us all, and we could say much more.

At the end of the Bible, when we come to the very last verses of Revelation 22, it is the Spirit and the bride who say, "Come." So, I think it is absolutely right that we speak of the precious oil. Where would we be without the gracious ministry of the Holy Spirit? There could be no repentance. There could be no faith. There could be no revelation. There could be no spiritual birth. There could be no union with Christ. There could be no changing from glory to glory, no transformation. There could be no enabling for the service of God. There could be absolutely nothing without this gracious and precious ministry of the Holy Spirit. The precious oil: that is the first thing.

The Anointed One

The second thing I want you to notice about the psalm is this: it is the high priest. Upon whom is the oil poured? Who is anointed with the oil? It is Aaron. He is anointed with the oil. Now, Aaron is a picture of the Lord Jesus Christ. Why does it say "even Aaron"? This little psalm was written probably something like a thousand years after Aaron, and yet it is "even Aaron." Why? Why did it not mention the high priest of the writer's day? He went right back to the very beginning—to the first high priest in the economy of God: Aaron. Although we know that the Lord Jesus' ministry exceeds by far that of Aaron, and is more like that of Melchizedek (and even that is only a pale shadow) yet we have here a wonderful picture.

What does the word *Christ* mean? We have altogether lost the very meaning of the word Christ. We speak of Jesus Christ, our Lord Jesus Christ. We say about Him, "Christ did this" or "He did that." But we forget altogether, even when we use the Hebrew *Messiah*, we still only think of it as the idea of some kind of great deliverer who is to come. But Messiah means anointed one and Christ is the Greek form of the Hebrew "Messiah"—anointed one!

The Lord Jesus is God's supremely anointed one. He is the anointed one of God upon whom the Holy Spirit came with absolute satisfaction—not because someone else had to die for His sins, not because He needed to be forgiven and made ready, but because of His own inherent and intrinsic worthiness. The Holy Spirit came upon the Lord Jesus as one who is absolutely worthy to be filled with the Holy Spirit—nay, to be the home of the Holy Spirit.

So the Lord Jesus is God's anointed one—anointed king, anointed high priest, anointed prophet. He is king, priest and prophet to us, the people of God. He is God's anointed one. There is such a lot of talk about, "Have I been anointed? Will I get anointed?" and all the rest of it. Forget it for a moment. You will never know anything about the anointing until you have got it absolutely clear first: *who* is the anointed one?

There is no such thing with God as millions of little anointings. There is only one anointing and the anointing is upon the head of the one who alone is worthy. No one else is worthy.

Can the Holy Spirit touch the flesh? We shall see in a moment. It is the one thing the precious oil, anointing oil, was not allowed to come upon—the flesh. If the anointing oil were to touch anyone like that, the true anointing oil, it would kill us. It would not mean life and transformation, but disintegration and destruction. That is what the writer to the Hebrews means when he says, "For our God is a consuming fire." We have lost the fear of the Lord in the 20th century altogether. We speak of God in a familiar way and think we can yank things out of Him, push Him around, shove Him about, hurl epithets at Him, as if somehow or other, the more like a salesman we are, twisting the arm of God, the more likely we are to get things out of Him. There is no fear of the Lord in that way in our eyes and that's the whole danger, unless you and I see that there is only actually one anointed one, and that one is the Lord Jesus Christ.

He is anointed because He is absolutely worthy. Not only was He born sinless, but He stayed sinless. Not only was He pure—that is, without sin—but He was positively holy. In other words, He went right through to the finish and proved that, although He was tempted in all points like as we are, yet He was without sin. The anointed one.

Well, here we've got it. "It is like the precious oil upon the head that ran down upon the beard, even Aaron's beard." Now, that is rather wonderful, really, because it just means simply that God has got the one who is worthy, and the one who is worthy is on the throne. The one who is absolutely worthy has come to the throne and has sat down. That is the next thing.

The Anointing on the Garment

Now, the third thing, which is all grace, the oil on the head runs down the beard to the skirt of the garment. Now, there is great discussion about the skirt of the garment. If you've got a revised version or a modern version, you will see that there is a lot in the margin. There are variations in the margin. It says, for instance, in the American Standard, "upon the skirt of his garments." I think in other more modern ones, it puts "on the collar." The Amplified gets away with it beautifully by saying, "the holy oil comes down the beard onto both the collar and the hem," and that is just what it means, because in Hebrew it is *the fringes*.

Now, the priestly garments had a hole, as it were, and there was no seam. There was just a hole for the priests head to go through. It was completely bound in blue and the hem was bound in the same way. So it's deliberately ambiguous; we have a deliberate ambiguity. Was it the collar? Was it the hem? It is the hem that it touches. What it means is this, it is the same thing: if it touches the collar, it has touched the whole.

Now you begin to see the whole glory of it. Because you see, this anointing which is upon the head of our Lord Jesus, which He alone is worthy to have received and obtained, is for us all. He has obtained the anointing for us all! The oil runs down and, as it were, encloses and encompasses, involves the whole body, every single member. Now, that is what this psalm is about.

Have you wondered why it says, "how good and how pleasant it is for brethren to dwell together in unity?" What's that got to do with oil running down Aaron's beard and onto his collar? What's that got to do with dew on Mount Hermon and the mountains of Zion? The whole point is that this little psalm is talking about all of us being in the body. Therefore because we are in the body, the anointing is for us all.

Now whether we have received that anointing or not is another matter. Whether we have recognised it, whether we are experiencing the anointing, that is an altogether different matter. But the fact of the case is this: that the anointing is there for every blood-bought child of God. Listen to this—this is the wonder of it. It is not given to you because you are wonderful and zealous and knowledgeable and all the rest of it. But it is given to you because of who the Lord Jesus is. Therefore, a person who is all the time, as it were, trying to be better, trying to be better, trying to be better and trusting in themselves to obtain something, will be disappointed. But the person who may be quite rotten and knows it, but sees suddenly that the anointing is there, won for them by Christ, and says, "Lord, I take it," that person receives it.

How many of our lives are explained by this? We all have deep down within us this idea that, somehow or other, although we have been saved by grace, yet we've got to somehow prove that we are holy, prove that we are really rather good, you know, the idea being that just underneath it is pure gold. The dirt is just on the surface. Scratch it off and you will find pure gold underneath. But this is not so.

Now, of course, we are not saying that there should be no zeal. We are not saying there should be no studying of the word. We are not saying there should be no discipline. We are not saying that there should be no purity. These things are right, but it is a question of whether we trust in them. That is why you can get a decent, respectable, knowledgeable person who is an old windbag, that is all, just a windbag. There is not a bit of life in them. They open their mouth in prayer, and it is just so many words. There is no life. But you get someone else who is pretty ropey, to put it in a slang term, pretty ropey, and yet when they open their mouth, there seems to be life there. You touch reality. It is this question of what we are trusting, who we're trusting.

Now, godliness is great gain when we don't trust in it as something in itself. When it can be the work of the Holy Spirit transforming us from within, then it is something wholly of God. It's not self-manufactured Christianity, but it is Christ-produced Christianity.

The Oil on the Head

The oil on the head—how wonderful that is. What that means is this: that, for every single one of us, there is a deep, real, and progressively fuller experience of the Holy Spirit. Or, if you want to put it another way, of Christ, and all that God has put in Christ for us by the Holy Spirit.

So if you turn to a few scriptures, we read in Acts 2:33:

Being therefore by the right hand of God exalted, and having received of the Father the promise of the Holy

Spirit, He hath poured forth this, which ye see and hear.

Who has received the promise of the Father? The Lord Jesus. Who has poured forth the Holy Spirit? The Lord Jesus. No fallen man can receive that promise. It is the Lord Jesus who has received it, because He alone is worthy. He has received it on the basis of a finished work—for us. That is, within the finished work of Jesus Christ there is something for every single child of God which the Lord Jesus has received. If you like, He is the custodian. He is the steward. Or, to put it in New Testament terms, He is the baptiser. He is the one who has obtained. Obtained what? Obtained the anointing oil, the precious oil. He has obtained it!

His name is like ointment poured forth. Not your name, not even your new name. *His* name is like ointment poured forth. He has received the promise of the Father. What is the promise of the Father? The promise of the Father is, "I will give them a new heart and I will put My Spirit within them." That was the old Covenant promise in Ezekiel and in Jeremiah. That is the promise that the Lord Jesus received. Now then, have you got it? Go back to Psalm 133. Who has been anointed? The Lord Jesus. Upon whose head? Whose head has received the oil? The Lord Jesus. Then see it: from Him it comes to us. Therefore, every single one of us can receive more of God through the Lord Jesus alone. He is the way, and the truth, and the life. No one comes to the Father but by Him.

Now, if you turn to Acts 10:38, here we have it:

even Jesus of Nazareth, how God anointed him
with the Holy Spirit and with power ...

God anointed Him with the Holy Spirit and with power. Now, it is the Lord Jesus, then, who, through His agony on the cross, has won for us this oil, this anointing of this precious oil. Therefore, there is no reason at all why every single one of us should not enter in, in an ever-deeper way, into all that God has for us. Why? Because it rests not upon our works, but upon His work. Not upon our worthiness, but upon His worthiness. The one thing that stopped you and I from being joined to Christ was sin and transgression. It was this that divorced us from Him. Now, on the cross, Jesus Christ not only bore our sins, but, like the scapegoat, He went out into the wilderness and carried our sin away over the horizon as far as the East is from the West. Our sin is gone, absolutely gone, blotted out. "Therefore there is now no condemnation to them that are in Christ Jesus." God has put us in Christ; no more condemnation. There is no reason, therefore, why we should not receive the oil.

Receiving the Oil

In other words, we may know that blessed ministry of the Holy Spirit. We may, at our birth (and some do at the very beginning, really enter into all that is theirs for them in Christ. But so often we do not. We come little by little. We are in the land, but how are we going to possess it? What is your need? What is it tonight that you need? Oh, if only God would give you faith to see that the Lord Jesus has obtained that for you. All you have to do is to rest on His finished work and enter in.

If you turn to 1 John 2:20:

And ye have an anointing from the Holy One, and ye know all things.

Now, isn't that beautiful, the way it is put so simply? Ye have an anointing from the Holy One. It is from the head to the members. Ye—each one of you—have an anointing from the Holy One. Verse 27:

And as for you, the anointing which ye received of Him abideth in you, and ye need not that anyone teach you; but as His anointing teacheth you concerning all things, and is true, and is no lie, and even as it taught you, ye abide in Him.

The anointing—there it is.

Turn back to II Corinthians 1:21–22.

Now He that establisheth us with you in Christ, and anointed us, is God; who also sealed us, and gave us the earnest of the Spirit in our hearts.

Now what I want you to notice is this: "Now He that establisheth us with you in Christ and anointed us is God." The actual word is "into" that is, we are being built into Him, growing up into Him, and He has anointed us.

The Result of the Anointing

Well, now go back to Psalm 133. Now we've got all that before us: this anointing, which is for every one of us. It's upon the head, comes right down to the hem of the garment. Now what is the result of this anointing? What should the result be?

Knowing the True Anointing

Whether we know the anointing in our experience or not, how can we be sure and certain that it is the true anointing, that it is of God? Well, there are three things in this psalm which always, infallibly, are the guide to any true work of the Holy Spirit. The first two we find in verse one, and the last is in verse three.

The first result is always unity. Oneness. "Behold how good and how pleasant it is for brethren to dwell together in unity." Spurgeon's comment on this was, "Yes, behold, behold, and behold again, for it is the greatest rarity in the whole universe." "Behold how good and how pleasant it is for brethren to dwell together in unity." It is like the precious oil. You can always tell strange fire because it is always divisive and always produces superiority. Always. That wisdom which is from below, of the earth, is sensual, devilish, and divisive. James 3:17 says,

> *But the wisdom which is from above is first pure,*
> *then peaceable, gentle, easy to be entreated ...*

and so on.

Now this is absolutely New Testament, because when we come to Ephesians 4:3, we read this little word: "Giving diligence to keep the unity of the Spirit in the bond of peace." Then that tremendous chapter unfolds. There is one body, one Lord, one faith; and so it goes on to a sevenfold unity. Then it goes on about how He's ascended on high, has led captivity captive, has given gifts to men, and then it goes on to the building up of the body to a full-grown man. Then he goes on, "From whom all the body fitly framed and knit together through that which every joint supplieth, groweth or buildeth itself up in the love of God." It is the unity of the Spirit.

Now let me be quite clear on this. The Holy Spirit brings a sword when there is any unequal yoking; believer or non-believer. Whether it be in so-called churches or anything else, the Holy Spirit brings a sword right across it. If there is anything which is sectarian in spirit, the Holy Spirit undoubtedly brings a divine veto on it. But the Holy Spirit's ministry is always to guard jealously the oneness of Jesus Christ. Unity, to God, is vital. This can never be overemphasised. It has been the devil's job and work down through the years to take things which are truly of God, and to steer them off the rail, and then to use them.

Here you have got it: "How good and how pleasant it is for brethren to dwell together in unity." How Scriptural is this? We have spoken of Ephesians 4:3, now turn to 1 Corinthians 12:13.

> *For in one Spirit were we all baptised into one body, whether Jews or Greeks, whether bond or free; and were all made to drink of one Spirit.*

Now am I to believe that there are two bodies of Christ? One body of those that are inferior and one of those that are superior? One that has had some kind of experience and one that has not? Or is there only one Christ? Whether or not some are inferior, and poor, and infantile, and poverty-stricken, yet still they are in Christ. Isn't that what the apostle means when he says,

"I beg you to receive one another as Jesus Christ received you"? How did He receive me? As a sinner, an unworthy sinner and we are to receive one another in exactly the same way.

We may yet, many of us, have many experiences of the Lord ahead of us, but never let anyone get away with any idea at all that any experience of the Holy Spirit, of Christ by the Holy Spirit, ever leads to anything but the building up of the body. That is why the apostle Paul went to such great lengths to express this when he spoke about tongues, prophecy or any other gifts. He said, "let everything be done to build up." If it does not build up, it is the surest indication that it is not of God. Now, we all know that in this world there is enough that is destroying. Here then, is one of the things of the anointing. "How good and how pleasant it is for brethren to dwell together in unity. *It is like the precious oil.*"

In other words, the Holy Spirit is the one who produces our oneness. He is the one who guards our oneness. He is the one who gives victory over the things that divide us. He is the one who makes the Lord Jesus real to us when we will temperamentally collide. He is the one who keeps us together when we are opposite poles in thought. It is perfectly true, as I have said, that the Holy Spirit brings a sword at times when it is a question of unbeliever and believer, or if it is a question of something which is dividing God's people, or hampering or hindering their moving on with the Lord. But let no one ever think that there is any other ground, that you can divide from any believer, other than this: that it is to be one with all saints.

Now, here is the second thing I would like you to notice, which is a result of this. By the way, there is another little scripture, 1 Corinthians 6:17, which puts it all so beautifully. It says,

He that is joined unto the Lord is one spirit.

It is unity all through. First of all, if you have any experience of the Holy Spirit, it brings you absolutely into a union with Christ. He becomes real to you. You somehow find yourself intimately bound up with Him. He becomes so livingly beautiful to you, so livingly near to you. Isn't it true that every time we have such an experience, we become humble? There is a humility that comes, a grace that comes, a brokenness which comes, which is so beautiful. It is ointment poured forth.

Well, now, if you turn again to Psalm 133, you will see that the second thing I want you to note is "how good and how pleasant it is for brethren to dwell together in unity." Now, it is one thing for us all to believe in oneness, but to dwell together, that is fellowship, isn't it? Not to allow one another to overwhelm us. To be ourselves, to be able to dwell together, not as all little Lances, or big Lances, but as each one, "I this, I that, I the other, I the other." In Christ, absolutely free, ready to be corrected by the balance of the whole.

Some people get so upset. Of course, the scripture says, *let us all be of one accord*. We are one. We are not always of one accord. But the scripture says, *let us have one mind*, and do you know, it even says *one soul*. That is the hardest thing in the whole world, for Christians to be one soul. But it says so in Philippians, one soul. Nevertheless, our basis is that we are one. Christ is our oneness. Now, here comes the liberation. We are not all to try and be like one another or all try to bow just in a kind of slavish way.

But we are just to be ourselves in the Lord, and to give room for one another.

In the church, there will always be extremes, but the mind of God is in between. Some of us temperamentally can only feel like John the apostle, and others of us are temperamentally more like Paul, and others of us are more like James. Even Luther had great trouble with James and Paul, and said rather rudely once, which he must surely regret now in the glory, that the letter of James was all straw and the best thing for it was to be used for heating the stove. He wrote that in his commentary. Why? Because, you see, Luther saw so clearly what Paul was driving at when he said "justified by faith alone," and he couldn't quite get hold of what James said when he said, "a man is not justified by faith alone, but by works also," and then went and committed the cardinal sin by giving two examples and saying, you see how a man is justified by works. It is all in the Bible, you know; all inspired. So shall we batter James into being a Paul? Or shall we batter Paul into being a James? Or shall we leave James and Paul in their respective places in the New Testament, and understand that the truth needs the whole and that no one brother or sister has got it all? Indeed, we have very little. We have very little. When we put the little that we have together, we have it all.

The Fellowship of the Holy Spirit

Now, that is fellowship. Fellowship is not all trying to be like so and so. Then it is no longer fellowship; it is an army and that is all. It is uniformity, regimentation. That is not the family of God.

The family of God is that we all grow up in discipline, disciplined by one another, having to take responsibilities, having to accept the problems created by living together. Yet, at the same time, we can all grow up originally, so that the Lord, in the end, can lead each one of us His way and blossom and flower and fruit through us. How important this matter is.

Now then, this is what the Holy Spirit does. Listen, "How good and how pleasant it is for brethren to dwell together in unity. It is like the precious oil upon the head that ran down upon the beard." Now then, is that New Testament? Well, let me give you a few scriptures. First of all, II Corinthians 13:14 (RSV),

> *The grace of the Lord Jesus Christ, and the love of God,*
> *and the fellowship of the Holy Spirit be with you all.*

It is the Holy Spirit who produces fellowship.

Now then sometimes people say to me, "Well, I can't have fellowship with so-and-so." Right! I'll tell you why, if you don't mind me telling you. I'll tell you straight to the face why you cannot have fellowship with so-and-so. It is because you are trying to grind your own axe, that's why. Any other brother and sister in whom the Holy Spirit is, anyone in whom Christ is, you can have fellowship with them. It is a question of whether you have got one note only to strike.

You have heard this story about the preacher. Two men were talking about their respective churches and preachers. One said, "Well, my preacher, he's only got two themes, all the time. We call him the ding-dong preacher. It's either ding or it's dong, but that's all. He plays between the two. Ding-dong, ding-dong, ding-dong." So the other said, "You should think yourself lucky. We've got only one theme, and all he does, he goes ding, ding, ding, ding." Now when we have only one theme, we cannot have fellowship with any others who are not on that wavelength.

But that is not fellowship. Supposing we were to treat our families like this. Suppose a father were to say, "Well, I am not going to have anything to do with my 18-month-old son, because he cannot discuss electronics with me. He is just not on the same wavelength. Of course not! Father gets hold of his son and clucks at him, and plays with him, and crawls on the floor with him. He is having wonderful fellowship. If his dignified business colleagues came and saw him crawling around, they would wonder what on earth's happening with him. He is so dignified, such a clever man. But he is having fellowship, family fellowship. That baby is his flesh and blood, and he's having fellowship. He is on the same wavelength.

So now then, the more you've got of Christ, the older you are in Christ, the more wavelengths you should have. It is a sign of spiritual immaturity when you can only meet people on one level. Service is to be able to meet everyone; it does not matter if it is a nun or a monk, if they are a Christian, but to be able to get it all through to them and have real fellowship on their wavelength in Christ.

Fellowship is a tremendous thing when it is looked at like that. That's why 1 Corinthians 1:9 says

> *God is faithful, through whom ye were called into*
> *the fellowship of His Son Jesus Christ our Lord.*

We are a body; we are a fellowship. We've each got a part to play. Some are young, some are old, some are dwarfed, some are ill spiritually. We do not just shut them out and say, we cannot have any fellowship. We have got to get down beside them and try to talk their language and understand.

I know someone needs to say all this to me at times, but the fact of the matter is, let us say it to all of us: it is the fellowship of the Holy Spirit. Isn't it beautiful that the apostle Paul in Philippians 2:1 and 5 says, "If any fellowship of Spirit ... have this mind in you." He begs them. He says, "If there are any compassions, if there's any fellowship of the Spirit." Oh, how narrow we are. How sometimes we whittle down this matter of fellowship to just our own little bee in the bonnet, our own little bit of Christ, our own little experience, as if that is the beginning and the end of everything when the family of God is so great. It was, I think, the secret of Watchman Nee's greatness as over against many others, that he could learn from the humblest saint; just to be able to come down to anyone's level and learn. How beautiful that is.

I suppose the people that have been the most help to me have been the people who really have had the most to give, but at times have come down to my level. Haven't you found that? When I say down, I do not mean they have lost anything. Far from it. They have come down to me and they've prattled with me on my wavelength, and I intuitively knew that they were like eagles flying away in the heavens. That meant more to me than all the great oratory I have ever heard, because it meant there was fellowship of the Spirit. It was communion of the Spirit. Someone wanted to help me. It is the principle of the incarnation. He being rich, became poor for our sakes.

Have this mind in you, which was in Christ, who, being on an equality with God, thought it not a thing to be grasped at, but emptied Himself, became a man, became obedient, even unto death.

Eternal Life

Well, there we are: Fellowship. Then, of course, the third thing about this anointing in Psalm 133 is life. Verse 3: "There the Lord commanded the blessing, even life forevermore." Eternal life. Well, now, that is always true of the anointing. The Holy Spirit; whenever He comes, He brings life. Why? Because if you read in Romans 8:2, "The law of the Spirit of life in Christ Jesus has made me free from the law of sin and death." That is what the Spirit of life does! He frees us from all these guilty fears, all this evil conscience, all this sense of condemnation, all this bondage from the past, all these things we carry over from the old life. He frees us again and again, progressively.

The law of the Spirit of life, the principle of the Spirit of life in Christ Jesus—there it is. It is the oil on the head, coming down the beard, flowing down to the skirts of the garment. The Spirit of life in Christ Jesus. Oh, how tremendous that is, when you start to think about it. Life, life, life. All the time, more life.

"If the Spirit of Him that raised up Christ Jesus from the dead dwell in your mortal bodies, then He that raised Him up from the dead is able to quicken your mortal bodies," it says in the few verses after that in Romans 8. Or again in Ephesians 1:19, "that you might know the exceeding greatness of His power to us-ward who believe, which He wrought in Christ when He raised Him from the dead and placed Him far above all principality and power."

The Dew on Mount Hermon

This is a very beautiful picture, this picture of the dew. Mount Hermon rises to some 10,000 feet, and it is in the far north of Palestine[1]. The mountains of Zion are in the South and when there is a cold air current sweeping down from the North, it carries the cold air from the mountains, and in the night, it quietly distils into dew.

Now, the mountains of Zion, I think most of you would consider hills, except perhaps the Danes. They would be hills to most of us, I think. They are not very large, not very high. Mount Zion itself is about 3,000 feet, but that is all. But the miracle happens every night. The dew from Mount Hermon comes to Zion.

Now, I think sometimes you and I would like something much more dramatic, much more sensational, much more noisy than that. But the work of the Holy Spirit—of the anointing, if you like—in another way, is not only so often to begin with a dramatic crisis, but then there starts this quiet, daily reviving, renewing, quickening, strengthening. In the south of Palestine, if it were not for the dew, nothing could live. So it depends upon the dew; the heavy, wet dew that comes from Hermon.

Well, now there are the three things by which we can judge the anointing, the true anointing: oneness, fellowship, life. If you

1 The land of modern Israel was historically called Palestine even years after the nation was officially established.

turn to Exodus chapter 30:32–33, [speaking of the anointing oil] "Upon the flesh of man shall it not be poured, neither shall ye make any like it according to the composition thereof. It is holy, and it shall be holy unto you. Whosoever compoundeth any like it, or whosoever putteth any of it upon a stranger, he shall be cut off from his people."

Now here is the law of the anointing oil. It is holy. That is, this experience of the Holy Spirit, this experience of Christ, is always to set us apart unto Him. It does not touch the flesh. That is why in Psalm 133 it says, the oil comes from the head, runs down the beard, onto the garments. It does not touch the flesh. It is a perfect picture of this law of the anointing, that the oil was never ever to touch the flesh.

Now, the greatest problem in any real experience of the Holy Spirit, whatever it is, initial or progressive, is the mixture between soul and human spirit; my spirit and my soul, your spirit and your soul. It is the mixture of the two things that is the greatest problem in the work and the service of God.

Dividing Between Soul and Spirit

That is why it says in Hebrews 4:12,

> *For the word of God is living, and active, and sharper than any two-edged sword, and piercing even to the dividing of soul and spirit, of both joints and marrow, and quick to discern the thoughts and intents of the heart.*

Now will you please mark this very, very carefully? *Dividing* between soul and spirit; not destruction of the soul. It is not the elevation of the spirit to the detriment of the soul. It is the dividing of the two things, so that one is set apart unto the Lord. Holy anointing oil shall not touch the flesh.

Our great problem is always our soul. Of course, we can get the idea from the word of God sometimes, and it is part of our religiousness (if you have a religious religiosity) that we have to suppress the soul. But a spiritual man is not a soulless man. A spiritual man is a man whose spirit is above his soul. You see, God's whole thought is a new man: spirit, soul and body. That is why it says in 1 Thessalonians 5:23 (see ASV and RSV), may the Lord "sanctify you wholly; and may your spirit and soul and body be kept sound and blameless at the coming of our Lord Jesus Christ."

Now, we all recognise that the body is a very important point, although some Christians let it go. They consider it as very, sort of, not spiritual. You are not spiritual if you care too much for your appearance. That is rubbish. Absolute nonsense. Your body is the temple of the Holy Ghost. So you must at least take a little care for it. One of the lessons I learned from Auntie Ella again and again when I used to say to her, "Take care." She would reply, "I do. Don't you tell me. My body has been bought with a price. It's a temple of the Holy Ghost." That is true. So wash it, keep it, look after it, dress it decently as far as within your income. Make yourself presentable and attractive. Don't ever think that spirituality is the letting go. That is mysticism.

In the same way, the soul is the means by which you and I communicate with one another. Now, as soon as you start to suppress your soul, you get artificiality and tension. Always. Our great problem is to get the origin, the seat of spiritual government, of the government of our being, out of our soul into our spirit. That is why the soul has to go into death, in order that it may come back into life in a new way. Do you understand?

The only way God can somehow get this centre, this headquarters, out of our soul—that is our will, our emotions, our mind—into our spirit is for us to know the dividing between the two. Sometimes it's a tremendous cost. The stronger the soul we have, the greater the personality we have, the more suffering there is in this matter of the soul. But do not ever come away with the idea that God wants soulless Christians. Far from it! He wants people who have souls released, so that for the first time they can relax. Now, the mark of a true spiritual man or woman is relaxation. Did you know that? Relaxation. They are just themselves, absolutely themselves. You can look into them and see all their faults. You can look into them and see the Lord as well. That is because there is a dividing between soul and spirit.

Now, it is very, very rarely ever talked about, this matter, and only the cross can do this work. Only the Spirit can bring the cross to us. Woe betide us if we try to take the cross to ourselves. But here it is.

No strange oil. It says in Exodus 30 no one is to ever compound anything like this or use it for any other purpose than that for which God intended. Then it goes on in the next little portion, if you were to read on, to incense, and it tells you about the incense, how it is to be. These anointed people are to offer incense upon the golden altar and the Lord says in verse nine, "See that no strange incense is offered." No strange oil, no strange incense.

Strange Fire

Now, people have asked me again and again to explain to them, and I have hesitated to do so—what is strange fire? The Lord has warned us a number of times about strange fire. But what is strange fire? Shall we all just go round with a great shadow over us? No. Let every single one of us seek to know the truth of what we have sung. "O thou who camest from above the pure celestial fire to impart, kindle the sacred flame of love on the mean altar of my heart." Let us seek for that more and more. Let us seek to know the anointing. Let us seek to enter into what is ours already won for us, and which is ours in Christ. But let us be very, very careful of what is strange fire, strange incense, strange oil.

The word *strange* in Hebrew means foreign and what God calls foreign may be something within us. In other words, anything that finds its origin in our soul or our spirit instead of in Him. Now, that may sound very complicated, but that is the root of the problem. It is the origin. Take strange fire, take God's fire: outwardly, they are the same. It is the origin. One came from God; one was produced by man.

If you turn to Leviticus 10, where you have this account of the strange fire, you've got Nadab and Abihu, the sons of Aaron. They were the two elder sons of Aaron and, if anyone had the right to offer fire on the altars, the incense on the altar, they had. These two were anointed. You read that in Numbers 3:2–4. It says these two, Nadab and Abihu, were anointed as priests to offer incense unto the Lord. So then, what were they doing wrong?

Why did they offer strange fire? What happened? They were anointed. They were the eldest sons of the high priest. They were priests. What was wrong? It seems quite clear to me that they got very excited by what happened in the previous chapter, Leviticus 9, when it says verse 24.

> *And there came forth fire from before the Lord, and consumed upon the altar the burnt offering and the fat: and when all the people saw it, they shouted, and fell on their faces.*

Nadab and Abihu took censers and went. They got so excited. This is always the thing with the soul, it overreaches itself—they went. It was the fire of God that destroyed the strange fire. Now that is a solemn thing, but that is exactly what happens. The true fire destroys the false fire. I have noticed, again and again, that strange fire always destroys. It always brings about this disintegration in the end.

Now, these men, as I've said, were anointed and so on. But do you notice in Leviticus 10:3, the Lord says, "I will be sanctified." That is why it happened. In other words, here it is, "I will be set apart." It is this division between soul and spirit again. The word *sanctified* is just divided, set apart. "I will be sanctified," saith the Lord, after these two had died, as an explanation of it. Then the second thing, you will see is in verse 7. The others, the other brothers, were besought to hide in the house of God. Security from strange fire was to be found within the house of God; within the church.

How? We do not always like being corrected or people sort of saying, "Well, be careful." We feel that they are just being dampers on everything. But you know, there is security in the house of God and I have found that even the poorest saints have a witness within them to what is of God. When you hear something that is of God, even if you don't agree with it theologically, you say, "That's right." You can't help it. Something in you just says, that is right. Condemnation is always the enemy's work, and whenever we have this awful feeling of condemnation, we must be very careful.

Well, there we are. There are many other things. That is strange fire. The anointing oil. It was because of the anointing oil. That is in verse seven too and you read that. Perhaps the Lord will give you a bit more light. But let us not just think about the negative side. Let us finish on this point—that our glorified, risen, triumphant Head has been anointed, and the precious oil has come down to every member of the body.

Every one of us has something to possess in Him. Have we possessed it? Are we possessing? Are we going on into everything that we've got? May God give every one of us help. What we need is sight, spiritual sight to see that it is ours in Him. Secondly, faith to take, and to possess what is ours in Him. "Behold how good and how pleasant a thing it is when brethren dwell together in unity. It is like the precious oil upon the Head that ran down upon the beard, even Aaron's beard, that ran down to the hem of the garment, like the dew of Hermon that cometh down upon the mountains of Zion. There the Lord commandeth the blessing, even life forevermore." May every one of us rise up and take what is ours in our blessed Lord.

Shall we just bow our heads?

Lord, how we thank Thee and praise Thee for what is ours in Thee. We worship Thee that, Lord, Thou hast obtained for us so much and

Lord, we can only say before Thee how saddened we are when we think how little we have possessed of what Thou hast so dearly bought for everyone. We pray, Lord, that we may have eyes open to see what is ours in Thee, and that we might know something of that anointing. Lord, every one of us. Thou hast said you have received an anointing from the Holy One. Lord, may we know that gracious ministry within us of Thy Holy Spirit, making real to us the things of Christ, enabling us to serve Him. Lord, we commit ourselves now to Thee, and pray, dear Lord, indeed, that that grace of our Lord Jesus Christ and that love of Thine and that fellowship of the Holy Spirit be with us all. Amen.

3. The Baptism in the Holy Spirit

I would like to take up this matter of the baptism of the Holy Spirit. It is, in my estimation, central to the gospel. It is a matter over which there is much controversy, much confusion, much perplexity, and to a certain extent, quite an amount of bickering.

You will find the words of John the Baptist in Matthew 3:11–12:

> *I indeed baptise you in water unto repentance: but he that cometh after me is mightier than I, whose shoes I am not worthy to bear: he shall baptize you in the Holy Spirit and in fire: whose fan is in his hand, and he will thoroughly cleanse his threshing-floor; and he will gather his wheat into the garner, but the chaff he will burn up with unquenchable fire.*

These are solemn words. Very important words. It is no good for people to try to avoid this passage as if it did not exist. I sometimes get the feeling in some Christian circles that they would really rather wish that this particular statement had not made it into the New Testament. But the fact of the matter is that it is not only in the New Testament, but it is right at the beginning of the gospels, and it comes in a statement which John the Baptist made concerning the ministry of the Messiah.

Now, my point is this: the heart of John the Baptist's ministry was illustrated, symbolised, set forth, however you would like to put it, in a baptism of water; an immersion in water. It was called *baptism unto repentance.* Everyone who hearkened to the voice of the Spirit of God, everyone who sought the Lord with a sincere and pure heart, John the Baptist commanded them, "Be baptised."

This is not what we know later in the New Testament as Christian baptism. It was a baptism unto repentance, but it symbolised the heart and core of his ministry. John the Baptist was given a ministry to prepare the way of the Lord and to prepare that way, he preached the judgment of God and the need to flee.

The evidence that a person really was moving in that direction was that they got baptised. Now, it seems very odd to me if then he goes on to describe something which is unimportant concerning the ministry of the Lord Jesus. If this baptism unto repentance was the heart of John the Baptist's ministry, surely he must be speaking about something which lies at the very heart of the Messiah's ministry.

He said, "He who comes after me shall baptise you in the Holy Spirit and in fire: whose fan is in His hand, and He will thoroughly cleanse His threshing floor; and He will gather His wheat into the garner, but the chaff He will burn up with unquenchable fire."

Now, is there such an experience as the baptism of the

Holy Spirit? Or should we put it another way? Is there such an experience as baptism *into* the Holy Spirit? I say unequivocally and as clearly and dogmatically as I am capable of, *there is*. Let no one make any mistake about this matter.

The details may differ from life to life. Some of our problem comes in bringing this whole matter down in such a way that we make it a technique, a series of steps, a method or something else. But do not let us get away. There is an experience of the Holy Spirit and that experience is vital and necessary to everyone who would be a functioning member of the body of the Lord Jesus.

When we turn over the pages to 1 Corinthians 12:13, we read these words,

> *For in one Spirit were we all baptised into one body, whether Jews or Greeks, whether bond or free; and were all made to drink of one Spirit.*

Some people have taught from this that only those who have a second experience of the Holy Spirit are in the church. I think this is quite wrong. It is unscriptural.

Others have taught from this that this is the proof that everyone who is converted is baptised in the Spirit. I think that is just as much at fault in that, because people say, "Well, you see, when you were converted, you were baptised in the Spirit." Well, theologically there may be *some* ground for that, but what does it mean to be baptised in the Holy Spirit? Does it not only mean that the Holy Spirit is indwelling us, but that also He is empowering us?

Now, I would think all Christians would say there is no argument about the indwelling of the Holy Spirit. The argument is over the empowering of the Holy Spirit.

My point is this: that no one can function as a member of the body of the Lord Jesus until they know both the indwelling and the empowering of the Holy Spirit. You cannot take part, you cannot contribute, you cannot participate, you cannot sense the mind of the Lord. All the time it has to be second hand. You leave it to others, as it were, to go ahead. Then you say, "Yes, I think that is right," instead of being able to be functioning members of the body of our Lord Jesus.

I hope that in speaking in this very simple way it may clear up for you some of the problems that beset us in this matter. You see, I think a lot of damage has been done by people who speak about receiving the Holy Spirit. I am personally not over worried about the technology of terms, because I know from my own experience that I was saved, but some years later I suddenly realised the Holy Spirit was a person. When that happened, something happened inside of my heart and it really was a receiving of the Holy Spirit. But He was there all the time.

So, I am not too worried about those who speak of receiving the Holy Spirit. But what does bother me is the kind of thought of, "I've got the Spirit! I was saved so many years ago, now I've got the Spirit!" Oh dear. I do not think that is a true baptism in the Spirit. You see, in my estimation a true baptism in the Spirit is that the Holy Spirit has got *you*. There is quite a difference, I think. When *you* have got the Holy Spirit, it is once again self-centred. "See me. I'm in. I'm sorry for you, but I may be able to help you with a few steps and methods. I may be able to get you in."

But it is "*I* have." What a different thing it is when, suddenly, the Lord Jesus takes someone He saved and He immerses them in the person of the Holy Spirit.

Immersion

I do not believe in sprinkling. I know some do, and if you are happy with that form of baptism, the Lord bless you. But as far as I can see, being buried with Christ in baptism—you do not sprinkle a few clods of earth on the coffin and go off and say, "We've buried them decently." You put them right under and the earth covers completely. That is why I believe in baptism by immersion. Not only because historically it is right, but because there was no other form of Jewish baptism in the New Testament other than baptism by immersion. They had no such thing as sprinkling. The fact still remains that it is an immersion.

Now, this baptism of the Holy Spirit—I prefer the term baptism *into* the Holy Spirit because that puts the accent on the right place. It is when the Lord Jesus takes *you* and immerses you into the person of the Holy Spirit.

Well, as far as I am concerned, I am all for that. I cannot think of anything more exciting, more wonderful! When we have found the Lord and we begin to get to know things, you know, and our heads grow in knowledge and we have a little experience of the Lord too, there is a sense in which we feel we are encompassing everything. After a while it all becomes stale and old, and we know it all, you know, especially you younger ones who have grown up in it; you know it all. You think, "So boring. There's hardly a song they sing that I haven't heard since I was a kid. And, you know,

I mean, they can't open their mouths and phrases don't drop out of them that I've heard since I was a babe in arms." Maybe there is slightly more modern language now, but oh, it is the same thing, we sort of feel we know it all.

What a wonderful thing it is when Jesus takes a person and immerses them into the person of God, the Holy Spirit. A brother called Him the Titanic Person of the Holy Spirit. Oh, I think that is absolutely marvellous. The one who brooded over the face of the waters when all was chaos and void and brought out of the emptiness, order, and out of what was not that which became substantial. I think it is wonderful when I see the end of the Bible, and I see those last words, "and the Spirit and the bride say, 'Come.'" The person of the Holy Spirit with the bride that from the very beginning of creation He has had in His heart, He knew that this was, as it were, the objective of all His working to produce this bride for the Son of God.

I cannot think of anything more wonderful. Oh, that this would start transforming our lives!

My word, to be immersed! Not just under the direction of the of the Holy Spirit, not just under the government of the Holy Spirit, but immersed into the person of the Holy Spirit. I cannot think of anything more marvellous! I know that theologically, some people will get a headache on this, but I often think of it like this: you see, when I was converted, it was the Holy Spirit that brought me to Jesus. But when I enter into this deeper experience of the Holy Spirit, it is Jesus who immerses me into the person of the Holy Spirit. Then we find the whole Godhead is at work; the Father and the Son dwelling in me through the person of the Holy Spirit.

Indwelling

Now, just to get clear on this matter, I think that Jesus made this perfectly lucid in what He Himself did and said in the gospels. For instance, you take John 20:21–22. This is the resurrection appearance of Jesus. You will remember that the disciples were there, except for Thomas. He was missing. This is what happened: "Jesus therefore said to them again, 'Peace be unto you: as the Father hath sent Me, even so send I you.'" And when He had said this, He breathed on them and they received the Holy Spirit. "He breathed on them and saith unto them, 'Receive ye the Holy Spirit.'" Then He went on, "Whose soever sins ye forgive, they are forgiven unto them; whose soever sins ye retain, they are retained." Now, I am interested in this because we know from John 7:39 that the Holy Spirit, though of course He was obviously in the world, was not given in the New Covenant sense of the word at this point.

Now, is that clear? It says, because Jesus was not yet glorified. In other words, Jesus had not ascended to the right hand of God the Father to sit down in glory.

So John 7:39 puts it quite clearly.

> *But this spake he of the Spirit, which they that believed on Him were to receive: for the Spirit was not yet given; because Jesus was not yet glorified.*

Now, I want to know what happened in that upper room. I know there are some who say, "Well, they did receive the Holy Spirit." I have questions about it, and I tell you why: because, when Thomas appeared a few days later, Jesus did not say, "Now listen, you have missed something which is absolutely foundational" He didn't breath on him and say, "Receive ye, Thomas, receive the Holy Spirit." He did not do it. He allowed Thomas to wait until Pentecost. In other words, it seems clear to me that it was Pentecost when the person of the Holy Spirit was given; that two things in one happened to those hundred and twenty. First, the Holy Spirit came into them and then He came upon them. At once. At the same time. Do you understand? Because it was the beginning of the age. So the Holy Spirit came *into* them and *upon* them.

Now, why did the Lord Jesus enact this little incident if it had no meaning? Surely it was for the disciples afterwards. Don't you think it was to make clear to the disciples? Never make a mistake—there are two sides to the Holy Spirit's work. One is that He comes within to dwell, and the other is He comes upon us with power.

Clothed

Now, you will find this in Luke 24:48–49.

> *Ye are witnesses of these things. And behold, I send forth the promise of my Father upon you: but tarry ye in the city, until ye be clothed with power from on high.*

Endued with power from on high; clothed with power from on high. Now, this is not breathing on them so that they receive the Holy Spirit within. This is a *clothing* upon them, something coming upon them. You know, clothing is a very important thing!

You may have the sweetest spirit in the world. You may have a degree. You may be a graduate. But if you are dressed improperly, you will be self-conscious.

Is it not true? It does not make any difference as to what degree you have. You may have done five, six years at university and come out with every qualification possible. You may be a doctor—not necessarily medical, but a doctor of some kind. I mean, you may have all the qualifications. You may have the most beautiful character in the world, but if the Queen asks you to have a meal with her and you went in grubby old jeans with a hairy chest bursting up like vegetation, I imagine that you might feel a little self-conscious when all the others come. Even if you might be a bit of an extrovert, I imagine that when, finally, in that daunting atmosphere, ushered forward by somebody to meet Her Majesty, you might suddenly feel all tongue-tied.

Character and degrees have nothing to do with it. It is clothing, is it not? Now, I know many people who are just like that when it comes to the work of the Lord. You see, they have got the spiritual character. Oh, there is no doubt about that. They have got spiritual character and they have got spiritual qualification too. They have been trained by the Lord; they have gone on with the Lord. But when it comes to it, there is a terrible self-consciousness because we feel somehow inadequate, as if eyes are looking into us, and in that moment, we are paralysed. We cannot function, we cannot witness, we cannot preach, we sometimes cannot pray, we cannot lead, we cannot do all kinds of things because somehow, we just feel unclothed.

Now, the Book says something about being clothed with power from on high. In Acts 1:4–5, in spite of the fact that Jesus, ten days previously, had breathed on them, and He said, "Receive ye the Holy Spirit," it then says, "being assembled together with them, He charged them not to depart from Jerusalem, but to wait for the promise of the Father, which, said He, ye heard from Me: for John indeed baptised with water; but ye shall be baptised in the Holy Spirit not many days hence."

Now, what do we make of all this? Well now, listen to me carefully in this: there is a definite experience of the Holy Spirit. I want to say this as clearly as I can on this matter. People sometimes charge those who have had a real experience of the Holy Spirit with sort of having it all. They say they have got it all. You do not need any more. Isn't that funny? Those who believe in another experience of the Holy Spirit say, "Well, of course. What is wrong with it?" They think they have got it all.

But the people who believe in the baptism at salvation say, "We've got it all. We don't need more. When we were converted, we got it all." Isn't it all childish, when you really think about it? Can anyone contain all of the Lord? Never. There must be more.

Now, there are initial things. You see, the Book speaks of two things. It says, in Ephesians 5:18, "be filled with the Spirit," and it goes on to say some very interesting things that I have often thought are overlooked because everybody naturally listens to this one wonderful and graphic command, "Be filled with the Holy Spirit." Verse 18, "Be not drunken with wine, wherein is riot, but be filled with the Spirit." But before then, it says this in verse 15: "Look therefore carefully how ye walk, not as unwise, but as wise; redeeming the time, because the days are evil. Wherefore be ye not foolish, but understand what the will of the Lord is. And be not drunken with wine, wherein is riot, but be filled with the Spirit." In other words, it seems to me that we cannot redeem the days, because they are evil. We cannot be wise and understand what the will of the Lord is apart from being filled with the Holy Spirit.

We shall be carried along by the sheer force of circumstances which the enemy will engineer in our nation. We will be worn out by this virus, and then that one, and then this circumstance, and then that, and then this problem, and then that problem. We started off so full of zeal, but after a while, we just begin to go on and we lose hearing the Lord anymore.

It's not that we're simpletons. It is the simple fact that only the Holy Spirit can keep us alive to God and sensitive to God and in a way of understanding. Then it goes on, "As speaking one to another in psalms and hymns and spiritual songs, singing and making melody with your heart to the Lord, giving thanks always for all things in the name of our Lord Jesus Christ." Well, I do not think anyone can be that kind of Christian without the Holy Spirit.

I mean, by nature, the very fact that we have got so much against us, so much pressure, so much conflict, is not going to help us to be all the time singing to one another in psalms and hymns and spiritual songs, making melody in the heart. That's a lovely get out, isn't it? For those who have no good voice. Lovely. It is lovely when people can sing beautifully and it is not so beautiful when people cannot. But it does not matter. The Lord says, as long as they sing, make melody with the heart. Then it goes on and says, "Subjecting yourselves one to another in the fear of Christ." I do not see how there can be any of this relationship without the person of the Holy Spirit.

Now, this to me, is not an initial experience because the word is, *be being filled.*

So my point is: the Holy Spirit may come within us, and does come within us at new birth. It is a question of the depth of our commitment and the measure of our obedience as to whether the indwelling Holy Spirit is able to do His work of producing real character in us. But there has got to be, at some point, a breaking of the spiritual sound barrier. Sometimes it does come when a person's born again.

I know one or two cases like that; it is very rare. I have to tell you that my experience all around the areas where I have gone is that it does not matter who it is. Nearly everybody at some later date comes into another and deeper experience of the Holy Spirit.

Once that initial sound barrier has been broken, then you must *be being filled.* It is a step of faith every day to drink more of the Holy Spirit, to take of that fullness, so that you are able to live the kind of life you ought to live.

I do not know whether what I am saying really comes home as it ought to. But you see, there is so much confusion on this matter everywhere.

I remember, years ago, I asked Mr. Sparks—because many people told me that he did not believe in the baptism of the Holy Spirit. Since the term was being bandied around all over the place, I thought, well, I'll get hold of him and I'll ask him straight, what did he think about the baptism of the Holy Spirit? I have never forgotten it. It was a great shock to me because I thought that he was going to say, "Oh, be very careful, there's no such thing."

But instead, he said, "Well," he said, and he thought, as many of you who knew him will remember, how he would for a while.

Then he said, "*Some* of those who say they're baptised in the Spirit have actually been born again."

That answered a lot of questions I had.

He said, "They were never born again." He said, "They were nominal Christians. They never had anything. Suddenly," he said, "the Holy Spirit's come inside and they live. But," he said, "you'll find those people don't have power." That answered an awful lot of questions for me because a lot of people who have said to me they had been baptised in the Spirit, still could not go out on the streets witnessing. That was very interesting to me.

There is no doubt that an awful lot of people have been born again. In Catholic circles, Episcopalian circles, Lutheran circles; everywhere you go, you find people who were converted in their minds. Suddenly, it's happened *inside!* Thank God for that. Then he said, "There is such a thing as a counterfeit. The thing is just psychic, where you get people, you know, doing all kinds of things to induce an experience, working up a kind of atmosphere where the thing is psychic." Yes, I had seen some of that, quite a bit of it. In fact, that was what put us so thoroughly off this whole matter in those earlier years in Egypt.

"But," he said, "There is a baptism in the Holy Ghost, and *that* every believer should seek."

I think Mr. Sparks himself was the living example of it.

Sometimes I go to some places and they tell me that Watchman Nee never believed in such an experience of the Holy Spirit.

I remember once talking with Ms. Fischbacher about it many, many years ago. She said, "Oh, he most certainly did. He not only believed it, but he had his own experience." Later on, Mrs. Stearns, Caroline Stearns in the States, said to me, "It was in my home.

We found him on the floor and had to leave him for a whole day." She said, "I've never forgotten the message he gave that evening." Now, my point is this: if you look into church history, there is no one who has been used of God upon whom the Holy Spirit has not come.

It does not matter whether it is Billy Graham—I am old enough to remember Billy Graham before his experience and afterwards. Oh, and I tell you, it is the difference between chalk and cheese.

I remember Billy Graham preaching up in Westminster Chapel when I was near to backsliding, and dear Arthur Matthews, assistant minister at Tewksbury, said, "Lance, would you come with me and my wife if we took you up to hear Billy Graham?" and I sort of said, "Oh, well, all right." I thought it was rather sweet of them to ask me to go, and I did. We sat there and I remember watching Billy Graham, this young man, very good looking, blonde, sort of going into the most incredible antics I had ever seen. He jumped over that rail in Westminster Chapel and rolled on the floor wrestling with lions.

He was illustrating the Christians dying in the arena at Nimes and honestly, you could hear the crunch of the bones and the *roar* of the lions and the saliva coming. I was all eyes and ears, and I thought, "What nonsense!" When it came to the end, when the appeal was given, there was this soft blues music in the background, you know, while the appeal was given.

Do you know, it helped me in this way that I—of course, I am a rather odd character—but the way it saved me was this: I thought to myself, there must be something in this. If a man goes to such extraordinary lengths to try and get someone saved, there must be something in this. Now, I was already saved, but I was very disillusioned. I was cynical, I was disillusioned, I was disappointed. My whole spiritual life had dried up. I was looked upon merely, virtually as a backslider.

Billy Graham himself said he had an experience after that.

When he came back, that next time, as all of you will know, there was a different man. There was none of all that sort of emotional thing. Of course, emotion was there. You can't preach without emotion. You cannot preach without a certain amount of acting. But the amazing thing was that now he stood and it was the word, word, word, word, coming up too. Then, when the appeal was given, thousands of people went forward, instead of just one or two people trickling forward and, you know, sort of urging them, and they sang *Just as I Am*, I do not know how many times. I mean, it was amazing. The man had an experience.

This was the same with Reuben Torrey. It was the same with D.L. Moody. It was the same with the Wesleys. If you go back into history, you will find it is the same with all. There is an experience of the Holy Spirit! For you younger ones, let me just tell you my own little experience. You see, when I was saved, I was saved very, very dramatically. I had what people normally associate with the baptism in the Spirit—visions and dreams and angelic visitation—all before I had a deeper experience of the Holy Spirit. It still did not do anything for me at all, because although I knew the Lord, I knew him outwardly.

I cannot explain it.

When I went to the School of Oriental African Studies and the full weight of university life came on me at the same time as being disillusioned with church life (at that time, we had two pastors and the whole church was ranged up between either one or the other in a great collision with fiery church meetings and I don't know what else) the bottom fell out of my life.

Then with the impact of socialism—I mean, I'd been brought up a good blue conservative and I began to think about not only socialism but communism. You know, one had to be honest. Those of you at university, you know just what I mean. You have got to open up, you have got that whole part of your life. You want to be absolutely honest, intellectually honest.

I wandered in this morass and I used to always be asking the same question, "But how? But how?" I used to hear victory preached from the pulpit morning, noon, and night and say, "But how?" Every time I used to say in my heart, "But how?" I used to look at all those faces and think, "Well, they've all got it but not me."

Then they used to sing hymns like, *My chains fell off*, and I used to say, "Well, my chains haven't fell off."

I did not dare tell anyone because I thought I was the black sheep. I found out later that all the other 399 had got chains on as well. But that was later. I mean, at the time I thought I was the only one.

They sang that line, *He breaks the power of cancelled sin, He sets the prisoner free* I thought, "It didn't work for me." Then Alan Redpath sent me a little booklet through the post. No big dramatics, no great lecture, just a little booklet, a little blue booklet entitled, *But How?* and when I saw this, *But How?*, well he must have read my heart! I never told him my "But hows."

It was God's timing.

You see, what I did was this, I thought, I will give the whole of Wednesday afternoon to prayer. So I went down to a little dusty, dingy parish church in Woburn Square and I knelt in that place and it was like heaven opened. I have never forgotten it. You see, what I lost later, due to some of the excesses I saw, which frightened me so that we drew back onto the more right but negative side was this: the first thing God said to me was, "The Holy Spirit is here … and He is here to take you over. He is in you, and with you, and He will reproduce the nature and character of Jesus."

Do you know, it was a revelation to me. I had never thought of the Holy Spirit as a person. I always thought of him as an *it*. He was always *it*.

He was always a power, a presence, an influence, a grace, a strength. I never thought that—just as you know Jesus as a person, just as you know God the Father as a person, you must know the Holy Spirit as a person. He is a person. He does not speak of Himself, but He's still the person of the Holy Spirit.

It was like a revelation. Do you know, I thought I'd never heard of the Holy Spirit. I must have heard many times, because the minister in the church I was in was a Keswick speaker. I mean, many times we must have heard the speech, but, I never heard it with my ears. Although he was preaching, it never went in. It just shows you how we take in what we want.

But when that happened, it was as if the whole Bible started to live. I said, "Oh, God, if I live and you use me to bring others to Christ, I will always put them in possession of a full gospel."

The second thing, of course, I learned that day was that I was crucified. That was as great a relief as anything else. I'd been doing my best to make Lance Lambert a good Christian. I'd been beating him into prayer, getting him into Bible study. I used to witness to one person a day. So I terrified the students at the school body, because I had that Wesleyan thing, you know, of buttonholing one person.

So, you know, as soon as I went in the student's common rooms as they used to be called in those days, I always had got a few spare seats, no matter how crowded the place was. They just went and I was left. I went down a corridor and people suddenly vanished into doors. That is the truth, they were terrified of it because it was not person-to-person evangelism. I got hold of them and said, "You know, I'm a Christian. Would you like to come to a meeting with me?" People were just terrified of it.

The greatest relief in the world to me was when I found that I had been crucified with Christ. I thought, "What have I been doing resurrecting that silly old Lance Lambert, trying to do so much with him when God has finished with him and put him on the cross?" Thank God for that.

Well, I remember that the Lord said a very strange thing to me when I got up from my knees, the last thing, it was like a person-to-person encounter with the Holy Spirit.

He said, "Now before you go, there's one last thing."

"Yes, Lord," I said.

He said, "No more witnessing."

I said, "Alright, Lord, no more witnessing until You give me the opportunity." For three weeks I lived for the first time in about four years. Instead of being a little spiritual machine, I suddenly sank back and became Lance Lambert. I enjoyed myself; I laughed, I looked at things. Suddenly, I found the places next to me were no longer vacated.

Now, my first experience, when someone came up to me and said, "Do you mind me asking you a personal question? What is it about you that is different?" A few weeks before, I would have told him in no uncertain terms, but on that occasion, I remember just saying, "Well, really, there's not a lot of difference, except for this major difference, that, by the grace of God, the Lord Jesus is alive in me." Then this fellow looked terribly moved, and his eyes filled with tears.

He said, "Well, how could He get into me?"

I thought, "Be careful, Lance. Must be the devil!"

I could not believe that anyone could come to the Lord as simply as that. So I thought, "Now you're being tricked. You're being tricked. Be careful."

So I said, "Well, you just open your heart."

"Well, where could I do that?"

"Well," I said, "you could do it here."

"Well, I will," he said and he did it!

I was flabbergasted. From then on, it was like a river beginning to flow. Up to that time, there was nothing. I was just a believer. Nothing happened, ever. I prayed morning, noon, and night. Nothing. But then it was just as if a great river started to flow; in one sense effortlessly, but on the other side at great cost. Because when the Holy Spirit really comes upon you in that way, when you are immersed into Him, then there comes the crisis of obedience.

It is one thing to say that you have been crucified with Christ, but another to come to the place where you have got to die.

Now, I have spoken a little more personally, but I have done it deliberately. *There is* an experience of the Holy Spirit.

If you get bothered about the terms, leave it. But there is an experience of the Holy Spirit. In my estimation, there is a baptism into the person of the Holy Spirit, and only the Lord Jesus can effect it.

The fact that He is the baptiser into the Holy Spirit is the most wonderful thing in the world. I want to come into His hands. I want to bow before Him. I want to settle the issue with Him. Since He died for me, since He has won everything necessary for me to know the person of the Holy Spirit, I want to. Don't you?

May God help us in this matter, to be clear in our understanding of this. Shall we pray?

Father, we pray that we may understand, as we have never understood before, the title of our Lord Jesus: that He is the baptiser in the Holy Spirit. Bring that home to us, Lord. We want to see the Lord Jesus as Saviour, and not only as Saviour, but as Lord. Not only as Lord, but as healer. Not only as healer, but as builder, and not only as builder, but as the one who baptises us into the person of the Holy Spirit. Lord, get down to those little blockages, those things that halt us, that paralyse us, that somehow, Lord, stop us from really entering into what Thou hast for all of us. We pray that those who are young in the Lord—that this word may be written on their hearts and in their lives and that they may, in Thy sovereign timing, come, Lord, themselves to know what we're talking about in original experience. We pray it for all. And we ask this in the name of our Lord Jesus.

4.
Some Thoughts on the Work of the Holy Spirit

Romans 8:1–30

There is therefore now no condemnation to them that are in Christ Jesus. For the law of the Spirit of life in Christ Jesus made me free from the law of sin and of death. For what the law could not do, in that it was weak through the flesh, God, sending his own Son in the likeness of sinful flesh and for sin, condemned sin in the flesh: that the ordinance of the law might be fulfilled in us, who walk not after the flesh, but after the Spirit. For they that are after the flesh mind the things of the flesh; but they that are after the Spirit the things of the Spirit. For the mind of the flesh is death; but the mind of the Spirit is life and peace: because the mind of the flesh is enmity against God; for it is not subject to the law of God, neither indeed can it be: and they that are in the flesh cannot please God. But ye are not in the flesh but in the Spirit, if so be that the Spirit of God dwelleth in you. But if any man hath not the Spirit of Christ, he is none of his. And if Christ is in you, the body is dead because of sin; but the Spirit is life because of righteousness. But if the Spirit of him that raised up Jesus from the dead dwelleth in you, He that raised up Christ Jesus from the dead shall give life also to your mortal bodies through his Spirit that dwelleth in you.

So then, brethren, we are debtors, not to the flesh, to live after the flesh: for if ye live after the flesh, ye must die; but if by the Spirit ye put to death the deeds of the body, ye shall live. For as many as are led by the Spirit of God, these are sons of God. For ye received not the spirit of bondage again unto fear; but ye received the Spirit of adoption, whereby we cry, Abba, Father. The Spirit himself beareth witness with our spirit, that we are children of God: and if children, then heirs; heirs of God, and joint-heirs with Christ; if so be that we suffer with him, that we may be also glorified with him.

For I reckon that the sufferings of this present time are not worthy to be compared with the glory which shall be revealed to us-ward. For the earnest expectation of the creation waiteth for the revealing of the sons of God. For the creation was subjected to vanity, not of its own will, but by reason of him who subjected it, in hope that the creation itself also shall be delivered from the bondage of corruption into the liberty of the glory of the children of God. For we know that the whole creation groaneth and travaileth in pain together until now. And not only so, but ourselves also, who have the first-fruits of the Spirit, even we ourselves groan within ourselves, waiting for our adoption, to wit, the redemption of our body. For in hope were we saved: but hope that is seen is not hope: for who hopeth for that which he seeth? But if we hope for that which we see not, then do we with patience wait for it.

And in like manner the Spirit also helpeth our infirmity: for we know not how to pray as we ought; but the Spirit himself maketh intercession for us with groanings which cannot be uttered; and he that searcheth the hearts knoweth what is the mind of the Spirit, because he maketh intercession for the saints according to the will of God. And we know that to them that love God all things work together for good, even to them that are called according to His purpose. For whom he foreknew, he also foreordained to be conformed to the image of his Son, that he might be the firstborn among many brethren: and whom he foreordained, them he also called: and whom he called, them he also justified: and whom he justified, them he also glorified.

I want to take a matter which I believe is very much on hearts today, and a phrase which we are hearing a lot about, and I want to investigate it just a little. I have entitled this as "Some Thoughts Upon the Work of the Holy Spirit." I say *thoughts*, because I would not want anyone to feel what I have to say is absolutely conclusive. But what I would like to do is explore an area that many people are talking about and which, I am afraid, is also a very confused area.

We find again and again that people who use the same phrases mean quite different things by the phrases that they use. Although there is a common phrase used, yet we discover when we talk with them that they have a different idea of what lies behind the phrase. I want to, as it were, provoke you to think. So please do not take what I have to say as conclusive or dogmatic. I shall make one or two very dogmatic statements when I feel I can be dogmatic. But you must remember that this, in many ways, is inconclusive. On the other hand, it may provoke you to study for yourself and explore in the word of God.

I have been looking at certain scriptures that I have known since I was saved. Yet there are things about those scriptures which I've never noticed before, things most provoking. There are some areas that I feel are almost wholly bypassed by many Christians. So, I want to provoke you to explore a little more of the work of the Holy Spirit.

What Is the Baptism of the Spirit?

Now, the first question I want to ask this evening is: what is the baptism of the Spirit? What is the baptism of the Spirit? This is a phrase that people use willy-nilly. We find that so many people use the phrase and have completely different ideas as to what exactly it means. Now, what is the baptism of the Spirit? What does it mean?

Now, let me say one word of caution straight away. Because there has been, in the past and is at the present, a certain amount of excess attached to the teaching of the baptism of the Spirit, many Christians have simply bolted to the other extreme and you discover that they will not so much as mention the baptism of the Spirit, as if it is a wholly and totally unscriptural phrase. I want to use the Scripture to underline that it is a wholly scriptural phrase and therefore should be rightly used. Of course, what we mean by that is another matter. That is what we will come to in a moment. First, let's look at all the scriptures that contain the phrase *baptism of the Spirit*. We will look at every one of them. There are not so many, but the ones that there are are important.

Biblical References to the Baptism of the Spirit

I want you to think very carefully as we read these. Matthew 3:11: "I indeed [said John the Baptist] baptise you in water unto repentance: but He that cometh after me is mightier than I, whose shoes I am not worthy to bear: He shall baptise you in the Holy Spirit and in fire."

John the Baptist, will you notice very carefully, is describing his ministry in a sermon. This is a message, if you look. When he saw these Pharisees and Sadducees, he defined his ministry, and he said it was a matter, essentially, of baptising in water unto repentance. But then he goes on to describe what is the heart of the Lord Jesus' ministry. Now, here is the important thing. John the Baptist, the greatest of all prophets and the forerunner of the Messiah, describes the whole work and ministry of the Lord Jesus in this one sentence: "He that cometh after me shall baptise you in the Holy Spirit and in fire."

It is as if John the Baptist was taking the final work of the Lord Jesus Christ—not just the work of the cross, but what the work of the cross was opening up: the possibility of the Holy Spirit coming to dwell within human beings. Tremendous. Now, do take note of that. I do not believe that John the Baptist was simply describing an aspect of the ministry of the Lord Jesus. He was actually summing up the whole work of the Lord Jesus. He summed it up like this: "He that cometh after me shall baptise you in the Holy Spirit and in fire."

Now, if you turn to Mark 1:8, we have the same record again.

I baptised you in water; but He shall
baptise you in the Holy Spirit.

Luke 3:16:

John answered, saying unto them all, I indeed baptise
you with water; but there cometh He that is mightier than
I, the latchet of whose shoes I am not worthy to unloose:
He shall baptise you in the Holy Spirit and in fire.

Every one of the Gospels has the record of this statement. In every Gospel it is at the commencement of the Gospel, more or less, as if it is the preparatory and introductory statement to the ministry and work of the Lord Jesus. John 1:33: "And I knew Him not: but He that sent me to baptise in water, He said unto me, upon whomsoever thou shalt see the Spirit descending, and abiding upon Him, the same is He that baptiseth in the Holy Spirit."

Now, those are the Gospels. Those are the only references we have to the baptism of the Spirit in the Gospels. Now if you will turn to Acts 1:5: "John indeed baptised with water; but ye shall be baptised in the Holy Spirit not many days hence." Now, this was the way the Lord Jesus described Pentecost. He said, "Ye shall be baptised in the Holy Spirit not many days hence."

Now, turn over to Acts 11:16, this is Peter speaking to the church at Jerusalem that was a little bit upset about his evangelistic meetings in Caesarea and Joppa. He says,

And I remembered the word of the Lord, how He said, John indeed baptised with water; but ye shall be baptised in the Holy Spirit.

Now, this is important because this reference to the baptism of the Spirit is a reference to the conversion of these men and women.

Turn back to Acts 10:44–47:

While Peter yet spake these words, the Holy Spirit fell on all them that heard the word. And they of the circumcision that believed were amazed, as many as came with Peter, because that on the Gentiles also was poured out the gift of the Holy Spirit. For they heard them speak with tongues, and magnify God. Then answered Peter, 'Can any man forbid the water, that these should not be baptised, who have received the Holy Spirit as well as we?'

Now, Acts 11:17–18. Now listen to Peter a little later when describing this incident where all those in this household were converted. Now pay very careful attention, because this is where prejudices and biases colour our whole outlook on this kind of thing.

If then God gave unto them the like gift as He did also unto us, when we believed on the Lord Jesus Christ, who was I, that I could withstand God? And when they heard these things, they held their peace, and glorified God, saying, 'Then to the Gentiles also hath God granted repentance unto life.'

It is quite clear in this particular instance, where the phrase *baptism of the Spirit* is used, that these people had a very deep and full experience at the beginning. They not only were justified and knew what it was to be justified by the work of the Lord Jesus on the cross, but they also had a very deep and real experience of the Holy Spirit. Now, I think, that's very important for us to understand.

1 Corinthians 12:13:

For in one Spirit were we all baptised into one body, whether Jews or Greeks, whether bond or free; and were all made to drink of one Spirit.

Now, mark it again. "For by one Spirit were we all baptised into one body, whether Jews or Greeks, whether bond or free; and were all made to drink of one Spirit."

Now, those scriptures are the total sum of the references to the baptism of the Spirit in Scripture. In actual words, there are no other references to the baptism of the Spirit. We will come in a moment to whether it's put in another way, but for the actual phrase, the *baptism of the Spirit*, that is all we have. From what we can see, we have to say that if we say that the baptism of the Spirit is merely to do with service, is merely to do with power for service, then we've got to ignore certain scriptures.

Similarly, if we say that the baptism of the Spirit is merely to do with regeneration, conversion, or the indwelling of the Spirit, the fruit of the Spirit, then we have to ignore certain scriptures. For in Acts 1:5 the Lord Jesus said,

> *for John indeed baptised with water; but ye shall be baptised in the Holy Spirit not many days hence*

Then a little later on, He said to tarry in Jerusalem until they received power from on high, when the Holy Spirit is come upon them and He said in Acts 1:8,

> *Then ye shall be My witnesses in Jerusalem, and in all Judea and Samaria, and unto the uttermost part of the earth.*

A Comprehensive Term

So it would seem also from Luke 24:49, that there is much to do with service in this matter of the baptism of the Spirit. In many ways, one would say that the phrase is very much related to service and functioning. Knowing that enduement with power from on high is necessary in order to be witnesses to the Lord, to serve the Lord, at home and elsewhere.

Now, there is much else we can say if we look at 1 Corinthians 12. Many have said, "Yes, well, when were we brought into Christ? When were we made members of the body of Christ?" "Well," we say, "when we were born of God." That is very true. That is when we first drank the water of life. That is very true.

But then, if you read the rest of 1 Corinthians 12, you will find all about the gifts and their functions. This is the point: it seems very clear and apparent from our general experience and the experience of church history that even if you are in the body, even if you are a member of Christ, you do not always exercise your gift. You do not always fulfil your ministry.

Now, what are we going to say then, about this term, the baptism of the Spirit? It would seem to me that it is a comprehensive term, describing the whole range of the Holy Spirit's work within and upon the believer.

Now, I'm not going to be dogmatic about that, but I suggest that it is a term, a comprehensive term, which covers the whole range of the work of the Holy Spirit from birth to glorification. The empowering of the Holy Spirit? Certainly. Absolutely certainly. The indwelling of the Holy Spirit? Yes, I think so, too. The indwelling of the Holy Spirit is needed for serving the Lord, and really knowing what it means to be one with other believers, to be built up with other believers, to be in the body. Yes, I think it is very necessary to have an inward experience of the Holy Spirit. When you are half-dead spiritually, you can easily sit in any congregation. But if you are alive with the life of God, you find some congregations very boring.

There is a sense in which your spirit is all the time reaching out for more of the Lord. You want more of the Lord. Somehow, something inside tells you that this idea of one man standing up and doing everything, and all the rest just sitting still, doing nothing is somehow wrong. There's more to it than just that. It's not "meeting-ality" or whatever you like to call it, just simply going to meetings and listening to someone preach, and so on. But it is a matter of *life*, of being in a body, in the body of Christ. If this is so, then, as I say, it's a comprehensive term, and indeed covers everything. It covers the indwelling of the Spirit, and the empowering of the Spirit; both the personal and the corporate aspects of our life.

The Essential Role of the Holy Spirit

I would like to say one other thing, which I think needs to be cleared up. Many of us are not theologians and that is quite understandable. Nevertheless, theology, real theology is, after all, only the word of God and we must understand this very simple fact: we cannot experience anything at all—upon this I am absolutely dogmatic, I will go to the stake on this point—we cannot experience anything of Christ at all without the Holy Spirit. This is absolutely important. It is vital.

Those who have shot to the other extreme and somehow or other, as the common saying goes, thrown out the baby with the bath water, those who have gone to that other extreme tend to say, "Oh yes, everything is all the Lord," and despise the work of the Holy Spirit. They pour scorn upon the gifts of the Spirit. They pour scorn upon the baptism of the Spirit. They so react against it that they are in danger of sinning against the Holy Spirit. It is a serious thing. I would say this evening that we cannot know anything of Christ without the Holy Spirit. How were you first convicted of sin? By the Holy Spirit. Not by a preacher, but by the Holy Spirit. You can listen to a million gospel sermons and they can go through one ear and out of the other, roll off you like water off a duck's back, unless the Holy Spirit takes one little phase and pushes it into the heart. Once it's in, it's in; you never get away from it. It's the Holy Spirit. How were you given faith? Faith is the gift of God. But how does God give us faith? Does He drop it out on us? No. The Holy Spirit comes with His gracious ministry and gifts faith, so that, for the first time, there is a capacity to believe. How are you born of God? You are born of the Spirit. You all know that. You are born, it's conceived of the Holy Ghost, and you are born with the Spirit of God.

We can go on, and we can show that we cannot glorify Christ without the Spirit of God. We cannot serve Christ without the Spirit of God. We cannot know the truth without the Spirit of truth. We cannot live the Christian life without the Holy Spirit. For the Lord Jesus Christ is still in His body—glorified, but located in a human body at the right hand of God the Father, wherever that may be. He is located at the right hand of God the Father. It is the Holy Spirit who takes the things of Christ and makes them live to me; who takes me and joins me to the Lord Jesus Christ; who actually unites us, so that it is impossible to know anything of God at all apart from the Holy Spirit.

This is what Scripture means when it says the natural man cannot understand the things of God. They are foolishness because they are spiritually discerned. They are discerned with the Spirit. As the Spirit of God works on our spirit, so we can discern and understand these things of God. Oh, it's a tremendous thing we're talking about, really.

The Fullness of the Spirit

Well, now, I want to move on to another phrase very closely connected with this matter of the baptism of the Spirit. If it is true (as I'm seeking to provoke you to explore for yourself the word of God) that this term, the baptism of the Spirit, really is a comprehensive term which covers the whole range of the work of the Spirit of God in and upon the believer, then let us look at this word fullness. The fullness of the Spirit. It is undoubtedly associated with it.

Filled With the Spirit

Turn to Acts 2:4. Now, this is the very occasion the Lord Jesus said, "ye shall be baptised in the Spirit not many days hence." Now it says,

> *And they were all filled with the Holy Spirit.*

This was the effect of the baptism. They were filled with the Holy Spirit. The baptism is really the fullness of the Spirit of God. They were filled with the Spirit of God.

Acts 4:31:

> *And when they had prayed, the place was shaken wherein they were gathered together; and they were all filled with the Holy Spirit ...*

Now this is very interesting. The same people who were filled with the Holy Spirit in Acts 2 were filled again in Acts 4.

Now isn't that interesting? Of course, there were many more added to them: quite a few thousand had been added in the intervening days. But it is interesting that, within a matter of a week or two, the people who had been filled with the Spirit in chapter two were filled with the Spirit again. So it is quite clear that this term *fullness of the Holy Spirit* is associated with the baptism of the Spirit and yet seems to have a slightly different view. Now, let us look at Acts 4:8

Then Peter, filled with the Holy Spirit, said unto them …

Acts 6:3:

Look ye out therefore, brethren, from among you, seven men of good report, full of the Spirit and of wisdom …

Acts 9:17:

And Ananias departed, and entered into the house; and laying his hands on him said, Brother Saul, the Lord, even Jesus, who appeared unto thee in the way which thou camest, hath sent me, that thou mayest receive thy sight, and be filled with the Holy Spirit.

Now, it is very interesting: he did not say baptised with the Spirit. He said, "be filled with the Spirit." Yet this was the first experience Paul, or Saul, ever had of the Spirit of God. Filled—that thou mayest be filled with the Spirit. Then if we turn to Acts 13:9, we read this:

But Saul, who is also called Paul, filled with the Holy Spirit, fastened his eyes upon him.

The Holy Spirit Fell on Them

Well, I must say then that it is quite clear that to be filled with the Holy Spirit is quite a normal occurrence in the New Testament, and that is very interesting. Now, there are also a number of times in the book of Acts where the term "the Holy Spirit fell on them" occurs. In Acts 8:16 it says of the believers in Samaria,

> *for as yet* [the Holy Spirit] *was fallen upon none of them.*

Then again, it says in the account at the centurion's household in Acts 10:44

> *the Holy Spirit fell on all them that heard the word.*

Did You Receive the Holy Spirit?

Again, in chapter 19, it speaks of them receiving the Holy Spirit. These people were not even saved. They said they had been baptised with John's baptism, because Paul asked them the question, "Did you receive the Holy Spirit when you believed?" Now, in the Authorised Version, of course (you often see it at Pentecostal churches written up as a motto), the Authorised Version says, "Did you receive the Holy Spirit?" Have you received the Holy Spirit since you believed?

Of course, that is interesting commentary on the change of language, because in actual fact, in the 17th century that meant, "Did you receive the Holy Spirit *when* you believed?" Nevertheless, the very fact that Paul asked the question shows you cannot be so clinical. That is a very interesting point, isn't it? "Did you receive the Holy Spirit?" Well now, what would you ask that for? Why didn't he just say to them, "Did you believe?" If it is synonymous—receiving the Holy Spirit with believing—then why would you ask this question? *Normally* speaking, receiving should be included with believing. If you are properly taught, you should receive, not merely believe.

I must say that in certain circles, I have discovered that because believing is made a tremendous amount of, and very little of receiving is emphasised, people are in fact justified—*how, I don't know*—and yet not really born of God! I believe it happens here in this country, too.

Nevertheless, going back to this point, we have to say, when Paul asked them, "Did you receive the Holy Spirit when you believed?" it is quite clear that in Paul's mind it was possible, although perhaps not normal, but *possible* to believe and not really "receive."

This I love, because it shows that Paul was a real physician and not one of those quacks. He didn't just have a few theories up in his mind that he just wanted to batter into people's heads, but he was interested in whether people really were in the *good* of the gospel and we have to say that.

So this is very interesting, the *fullness of the Spirit*, and these other terms that we find. That, by the way, is Acts 19:2.

> *and he said unto them, Did ye receive the Holy Spirit when ye believed? And they said unto him, Nay, we did not so much as hear whether the Holy Spirit was given.*

That's the state of these folk. Of course, they were not believers, so they believed, they were baptised, and the Holy Spirit, it says, came on them. This is another current use of this word. We can say fell on them or came on them. Now, these are all very interesting phrases and they all reveal aspects of the work and ministry of the Holy Spirit. Receiving, coming within and coming upon. Within and upon. These are the two sides of the Holy Spirit's work, His indwelling and His empowering: within and upon.

If you think of those two little phrases, *coming within* and *coming upon* you will discover you have the whole work and ministry of the Holy Spirit in a nutshell. Or if you like, you can think of it as *within and behind*, in the sense of someone driving you along like wind in your sails, blowing you forward. But the idea is upon, as it were; absolute coming upon someone with power, so that they are enabled to live the Christian life.

Filled Unto all the Fullness of God

Now, in this matter of the fullness of the Spirit, I think we should take note of two scriptures. Ephesians 3:19:

> *and to know the love of Christ, which passeth knowledge,*
> *that ye may be filled unto all the fullness of God.*

I have always been amazed by this phrase, "ye may be filled unto all the fullness of God." This, of course, is quite honestly impossible. I mean, it will take the whole church to be filled unto all the fullness of God, and even then there will be oceans unexplored. You just cannot comprehend. You cannot talk about boundaries to God. God is infinite. There is no end to God. There are no boundaries. Even if you were to journey a million, million years, a billion years, trillion, or whatever you call them beyond that—you cannot come to the end of God. God is infinite. There are no boundaries to God. There's no end to God. Yet it says here, filled unto all the fullness of God. People (sometimes even Christians!) tell me that they think it might be boring in heaven. I can't see how it can be boring in heaven, if there's all that to be explored. Even when we've explored so much, we can't come to an end of it. I should think by the time we've explored a bit more, we shall have forgotten what we explored back there and we will have to go back and have another look at it. I don't know. I only know myself that when I leave some place that I've seen, I sometimes have a longing come over me to go back and have another look at it. I don't know what it will be like in the glory, but here it says that we are to be filled in the end, "Ye may be filled unto all the fullness of God." How? By knowing the love of God, that is how. By experiencing the love of God in every way, we shall, in the end, be filled unto all the fullness of God.

Now, this fullness of God—how are you filled to the fullness of God, may I ask? By sitting in your chair, singing a little hymn from the redemptional Keswick Hymn Book as the mood takes you? Or the supplement, if you feel that way inclined? How are you filled unto all the fullness of God? Do you get filled unto all the fullness of God by uttering a few sweet little prayers, either from the prayer book or extempore according to your traditional background? How do you get filled unto all the fullness of God? Do you get filled unto all the fullness of God by trying? How? There is only one way you can be filled to the fullness of God: by being filled with the Spirit. That's the only way. There is absolutely no other way. The link between being filled unto all the fullness of God is the Holy Spirit.

Now, if you turn over the pages to Colossians 2:9–10, we read this:

> *For in Him* [that is, in Christ] *dwelleth all the fullness of the Godhead bodily. And in Him, ye are made* [complete or] full, *who is the head of all principality and power.*

This is the fullness of Christ.

Now, in Colossians 3:11, it speaks of Christ filling all in all, and the same in Ephesians 1:23. Well, what does it all mean? How can I know Christ filling all in all? How can I be made full in Christ, who is the fullness of the Godhead? By only one way: not by wishful thinking; not by trying; not by knowledge; but by an experience of the Holy Spirit.

This simply means that if you and I are ignoring the work and ministry of the Holy Spirit, we are cutting ourselves off from fullness. It's as simple as that. You can have all the knowledge in the world, so that from heaven's point of view you have a head seven times the size of your body, filled with knowledge. You can read every book available on Christian doctrine, Christian life and service, go to all the right missionary meetings and support all the right missionary societies. But if you haven't got an experience of the Holy Spirit, you are absolutely divorced from the fullness of God and of Christ. Absolutely divorced. There is an inseparable and impassable gulf between you and the fullness of God in Christ, because the bridge is the Holy Spirit. Now this I am saying very definitely. I said I hope you wouldn't take me as conclusive on all these things, but I did tell you I'd be dogmatic on the things I think we can be dogmatic on.

Sealed With the Spirit

Now, before I pass on to another question, there are a few scriptures, I would like you to look at. These are the scriptures I believe are totally ignored by many Christians. First of all, look at Ephesians 1:13–14. Now, I want to provoke you once more to go away and think, really think. Now listen:

> *In whom ye also, having heard the word of the truth, the gospel of your salvation—in whom, having also believed, ye were sealed with the Holy Spirit of promise, which is an earnest of our inheritance, unto the redemption of God's own possession, unto the praise of His glory.*

Sealed with the Spirit, who is an earnest.

Now, if you turn over to Ephesians 4:30:

> *And grieve not the Holy Spirit of God,*
> *in whom ye were sealed ...*

Now, I'm very interested in this word, "In whom." In whom ye were sealed. This is the same thought as baptism! Immersed in the Holy Spirit, you see? *In* Him. You see this little phrase, "in Christ," what does it mean? How can you be in Christ? The only way you can be in Christ is to be in the Holy Spirit. When you step into Christ, it is the Holy Spirit here, who makes it a living reality. In whom ye were sealed. "Grieve not the Holy Spirit in whom ye were sealed unto the day of redemption." That is marvellous, isn't it?

Then turn back to II Corinthians 1:22:

Who also sealed us and gave us the earnest of the Spirit.

Now it actually says, "anointed us," "sealed us," "gave us the earnest of the Spirit." Now, this is very interesting because these are words that are very rarely ever spoken about. Sealed; this is a very interesting word. It means to seal up. The idea is a letter or a document, where a signet ring is taken by the writer or the authoriser, and in wax he stamps it, he seals it with his seal, and he sends it by a special messenger, and no one is allowed to open or break that seal. Now, the same idea is in the book of Revelation where it speaks of that little book sealed with seven seals. Each one is sealed with the signet ring of God. Who is the signet ring of God? Who is the signet ring of God in whom ye were sealed? The Spirit of God is the signet ring. He is the One who transmits the authority of a risen Christ and seals us. It is as if He's saying, "Now then, you are a living epistle and you are sealed up to the day of redemption. All that I've got in there is sealed up. There's the wax, and there's the seal." Do you see?

Now, a seal is something evident. So don't think that it's not evident. A person who's going to seal something doesn't do it on the inside; he does it so that it can be clearly seen whose seal it is. This is so with the sealing of the Spirit. That's why it has got to do with the baptism of the Spirit. Again, it is this thought of the empowering of the Spirit: there is something manifest in your life, that you're seeing there is an absolute imprint on your life. There is something which is like a seal. It is there for all to see.

This person has been authoritatively taken hold of by God and the seal is there for all to see, and also for the devil to see.

The devil only comes round, has a look, and he sees the seal. Oh, he can't do anything; can't tamper with that seal. That seal is the seal of God. He dares not tamper with the seal. He can only get us to ignore all that altogether and walk into his hands so that he'll get us, but the seal is there.

The Earnest of Our Redemption

Now, what is this word *earnest*? Well, again, I think you have heard this wonderful word earnest. For those of you who do this kind of thing, it is when you go into a shop and you see something you like very much, "Oh, I'm so sorry, I haven't brought my money with me." A person who's very wise, especially if they're Jewish, will say to you, "Well, a deposit will secure it." So you fish into your purse and you say, "Well, how much?" And they say, "Well, it's five pounds. If you'll put ten shillings deposit on it, it's yours. We keep it till you come and collect it."

This is what the word earnest means. It really means earnest money, or caution money. The idea is that here is something no one else is allowed to tamper with. It's purchased. When God gave us the Holy Spirit, the Holy Spirit in us is the earnest of our redemption. Isn't that marvellous? It means that God's got a deposit in us. Now, this is very wonderful, because it means there's much more to come.

So if we've tasted of the Holy Spirit down here and of Christ down here, and it's absolutely glorious, just think what it's going to be up there! People say it'll be boring? I mean, we shall run round in circles with joy! Just the very thought of it—a taste of it down here transports us into glory with all our aches and pains, and the devil, and spirits, and the world against us, and our own temperament, and misunderstanding Christians, and much else. Think up there in glory, what it will be like when we've left all that behind and we shall just be absolute. Now is only the earnest, only the deposit. One day, we're coming into the full thing. It's as if the Lord has said, "Now then, on that person, I've put a deposit; I want that one".

So when the Lord Jesus comes in the clouds to take us to Himself, that will be the day of the redemption of our body. Oh, wonderful. A new body. The Lord will say, "Don't anyone touch that one or that one. Whether they're in the grave or not, it doesn't matter." If we're alive, it'll be wonderful to see the Lord come. But if we're in the grave, it won't matter at all.

Won't it be marvellous just to see that day? Often, I wonder what's going to happen in some graveyards. I suppose I've got a macabre sort of interest to see what will happen in that day, when somehow people come out of all kinds of places and go up to meet the Lord in the sky. Won't it be a wonderful day? The redemption of the body. We'll have new bodies. It's not so strange as it sounds because, after all, when our bodies are decayed, the actual atoms are still there somewhere. It just means the Lord has to bring them back and re-form them. Then there they are again, a new redemption body.

It won't be the same as the old body, and yet it will be. I believe there will be something we should be able to recognise. But we're straying from the subject.

There's a deposit on us. It is as if the Lord said, "Look at that poor, ugly old creature down there. I put a deposit on him or her. I know she's not much to look at, or he's not much, but nevertheless, I put a deposit on him. Though there's sin in his body or her body to the end of her days and though she'll know tribulation in this world, I've put a deposit on that one. Not only in the spirit, not only in the soul, but in the body. Every hair of the head numbered."

Every hair of the head numbered. Even when they fall out. They must be re-numbered every day. The Lord knows it all. Then one day, when we're in the glory, every bit of it will come back. Every bit of it. It's a wonderful thing. There's an earnest. An earnest has been put on, and we are sealed with a seal, and there's a deposit being put on us. It's the most glorious thing. Dear child of God: it's all to do with the Holy Spirit. It's all to do with the Holy Spirit. Woe betide us if there's no seal, if there's no earnest. Do you see? What would have happened to those Ephesian believers if they just believed and yet there was no Spirit? No seal, no earnest, no bridge into the fullness of God. How foolish we are when we despise these things.

The First Fruits of the Spirit

Then we come back to Romans 8:23. I want you to see that Romans 6 may be a wonderful chapter, as are Romans 3, and 4, and 5, but it is the Holy Spirit that in the end is the key to a living, practical experience. Romans 8:23:

> ... *ourselves also, who have the first fruits of the Spirit* ...

We've got the first fruits of the Spirit. Again, it is the same thought: we've only got the beginning. The first flower has blossomed.

You know, when you go out into the garden in the first part of the early summer, you see the first roses and you think, "There's the first bloom." The first bloom is blooming. What's going to come? A great mass of colour is going to come after that and so it is with the Holy Spirit. We've got the first fruits. Something's happening inside of us and it's first fruits. There's a tremendous amount more to come.

When Do We Experience the Baptism and Fulness of the Spirit?

Well now, that was my first question, which has taken quite some time. My second question is, when do we experience the baptism and fullness of the Spirit? Now here I'm going to be most inconclusive. Theologically, it is when we are born of God. Experientially, it is when we appropriate it by faith. That is the only way that we can decide when a person really knows the baptism of the Spirit.

Now, of course, I'm talking of the baptism of the Spirit in its fullest range. There are aspects of the work of the Holy Spirit which may well come afterwards. The Lord Jesus was born of the Holy Spirit. Thirty years later, He was endued with power. He was anointed for His service. People call that the baptism. I wonder whether they can, it's certainly not scriptural. But He Himself described it as anointed. He said, "I am anointed to preach good tidings." That's how He described it. And anointing, of course, is for service. It's all to do with enduement of power for service. Well, now all that is important. Everything may be ours, offered to us by God through Christ, but our eyes may not be opened to what is ours, to what is offered, and therefore we may not have possessed it by faith. It's all very well to say everything is ours. Of course, everything is ours. But I mean, if our eyes haven't opened to what is ours, we can live in the midst of luxury and be ignorant. We can live in the midst of plenty and be poor. Our eyes have got to open. Not only have our eyes got to open, but we've got to have faith, which sees all this provided and knows we can take it, as much as we want.

Living in Our Own Strength

Let me illustrate. We talk about being crucified with Christ. I know so very few people who, at the very beginning of their Christian life, when they were born of God, really entered into an experience of being crucified with Christ. We speak of the indwelling of Christ. How few believers, really, at the beginning, enter into an experience of the indwelling of Christ. I know myself, for six years, I had no idea that we were crucified with Christ! It would have saved me a lot of problems if I had. I had no idea that I was indwelt by the Holy Spirit; had no idea. So it is with many of us.

Some people go almost a lifetime. They're Christians, and yet they never know that they've been crucified with Christ, or that the Holy Spirit is really within them. It's not a practical, living reality and experience. So it can be with the empowering of the Holy Spirit: we can go through life, you know, trying, somehow or other, to do everything.

It reminds me of a thing we once saw in the East: an old bus with two oxen in front of it, pulling it, because the man evidently either had lost the engine or didn't know what petrol was, so he had two oxen in front pulling the bus. I often think this is like us. We've got the engine, but we ignore altogether both engine and fuel, and we pull it along with our own energy, doing our best, somehow or other, to live this Christian life. It is all our own resources and energy.

Well, I think we must say, as I've already pointed out, we cannot be clinical about these things. The baptism is an initial experience. When I say initial, it can be at the very beginning of our Christian experience, or it can come from much later. But it's an initial experience. The fullness of the Spirit is a daily experience, or ought to be. The reason why some people have an experience of the Holy Spirit and then later on are right back where they started, is because they have not understood that one experience will not last forever. One experience shoots us, as it were, into a new dimension, to a new realm. From then on we must learn day by day to appropriate. We must be filled.

That's why in the book of Acts, you'll find they're filled, and filled, and filled, and filled again. They need to be filled continually. We need to be filled continually. Now, let me just underline one more thing before I go on to another question. We must never let theory or even icily correct theology hold us back from experience in what we believe. I believe it is the devil's masterpiece in cunning that he has managed to use truth to hold back multitudes of believers from experiencing what they believe.

Oh, you say to them, "Why don't you seek the Holy Spirit?"

"Seek the Holy Spirit? I have the Holy Spirit." Yet it is perfectly apparent from their lives that the Holy Spirit is absolutely absent!

If you get them right onto the basis of honesty, they will tell you, yes, they are fearful. They are bound. Yes, they know it. And so on and so forth. Oh, no, they couldn't do that. No, they couldn't do this thing or that thing, and so it goes on. They can't do it. "But you say, you have the Holy Spirit?" "Oh, yes." Now, what's wrong?

Truth is holding them back from entering into an actual experience of what they believe. Oh, they couldn't possibly seek. That would be quite wrong, to seek something they have already got. Well, then I suggest something else just as good as seeking. Ask the Lord to open your eyes to what you've got. That's all. Just ask the Lord. I believe the Lord doesn't notice too much of our phraseology. When He sees someone seeking, He says, "Oh, that's wonderful. They've already got it. But now I can show them. Because they're seeking; they're being honest. They know that there's a lack somewhere in their life." Well, I think this is very important indeed.

In our hearts, we know whether we're experiencing or not. Every single person reading these words knows in his or her heart whether they're really experiencing what I'm talking about. Whether you know what it is to be sealed with the Holy Spirit. Whether you know what is to be being filled all the time with the Holy Spirit. You know what it is to be baptised with the Spirit. You know what it is to be joined to the Lord, to be lost in His fullness. You know what it is to be clothed with power from on high, and so on and so forth. You know it, or you don't know it. Don't let doctrine, even true doctrine, hold you back from coming into the experience of what you actually believe.

Our Needs and God's Provision

Now, the third thing I want to look at is what is our need and what is God's provision in the Holy Spirit? Now, of course, this could be a whole evening study alone. But I want to take four scriptures, four scriptures alone and from them I want to point out our need, and then I want to show you God's provision in the Holy Spirit. Now, this might help us to know whether we have a real experience of the Holy Spirit.

Are You Naked?

The first scripture is Luke 24:49:

> *And behold, I send forth the promise of My Father upon you: but tarry ye in the city, until ye be clothed with power from on high.*

Now, in the American Standard Version, in the Revised Standard Version, it is "clothed with power from on high." In the Authorised Version, it is "endued with power from on high."

Now I want to speak about your need. What is your need? Well, now, is your need, can I put it this way—now, think carefully—is your need clothing? Think. Is your need nakedness? Oh, yes, you're a child of God. You're born of His spirit, but you're naked. Well, now, look, let me ask you a few other questions. We'll soon find out whether you're naked spiritually or not. Because the Lord once said to the church at Laodicea, "... and knowest not that thou art naked." I wonder if the Lord looks at you and says, "You've got no clothes on." You've got no clothes on. Spiritually, you're naked, absolutely naked.

Well, let me put it this way. Are you self-conscious? Self-conscious to the degree, spiritually, that you're paralysed when it comes to doing anything? You're full of fear, so that when it comes to prayer, you can't really pray; not freely. When it comes to praise, you can't really praise spontaneously. When it comes to witnessing, you're in a terrible state. The result is that when you do witness, it comes out like a cork out of a bottle, just about to explode, with the result that people tend to stand back rather in horror, instead of it being a natural, spontaneous, normal thing, as it ought to be.

Now, are you naked? I've often heard people put it like this: they say, when they're asked to go somewhere, "Oh, no, I couldn't go. I'm not properly dressed." Not properly dressed. I wonder whether that's how you feel about the Lord's service. "No, no, I couldn't, I couldn't. I'm not properly dressed. I just couldn't do that." You see, really what you're saying is, "I'm naked" or "what I've got on is so poor that I couldn't do that."

You perhaps have a kind of shame, which goes for humility; the kind of thing the Bible calls hanging the head. You know, it's a kind of thing that some people think is humility. It's not humility at all, of course, it's a terrible thing. It's not your fault, necessarily. It's because you're naked. You see, you're naked.

So what is the Lord's answer to this? Well, here it is: "Clothed with power from on high." Clothed! Absolutely clad. Clad in such a way that you're no longer self-conscious. Of course, everyone's rightly self-conscious in a way, otherwise we'd be unbearable. I mean that we haven't got the kind of self-consciousness which robs us of all our joy and peace and spontaneity. We can be normal. You can actually be normal because you're rightly clad.

I remember once I came to a meeting all dressed in a black suit, ready for the evening service. I'd been a bit absent-minded, dashed out, and came. Just as I was getting up to come downstairs, I looked down and on my feet were the most terrible old pair of brown shoes I'd ever seen. I don't know whether it was pride or what it was, I was so taken back, I thought, well, I can't preach in that. It would just finish me off. So someone had to cycle over the bridge as quickly as they possibly could and get my black shoes and bring them swiftly back. You see, it was just self-consciousness. I just thought, how could I do that?

It's rather like going to a certain sort of affair, and you know that they're all going to dress in a certain way, and you haven't got the right suit or something else. You say, "No, I'd rather not go," because you're self-conscious.

The scripture says, "Ye shall be clothed with power from on high." Wouldn't you like that? Now, just forget Pentecostalism. Just forget all the excess that there is so often. Wouldn't you like to be clothed with power? Wouldn't you like—not to be like a great loud Boeing 707 roaring through the sky—but to just be a normal average Christian? When I say a normal average Christian, I don't mean the normal average Christian by what we've got, but by what God means. A really normal average Christian. A person who can smile. A person who's got joy when everything goes wrong.

A person who's got peace in deepest distress. A person who's not nagged by fear, warped and embittered by the past.

Oh, my. Wouldn't you like to be clothed? A lot of our troubles come because we think people will find us out. Why? Because we're frightened they'll see our nakedness. If only we could be clothed, rightly clothed. It would be a wonderful thing, wouldn't it? Do you know what the word actually means? It means this: to enter into us a garment or to cause to go into us a garment. That's rather like the mother pushing her little boy into a coat and into his trousers. See, she's pulling them on. In the middle voice, it means to be clothed upon. But the idea is of stepping into clothes, you see. This is what the Lord says: "Ye shall be clothed with power from on high." There'll be something round about you.

Adam and Eve in the garden had a glory covering, so they were completely uninhibited, and quite spontaneous and free. So we, as Christians, spiritually ought to be clothed with the power of God so that we can be ourselves in God. So that we can just be quite normal. So that we can function. Well, I think that's a wonderful thing.

Are You Empty?

If you'll turn to Ephesians 5:18:

> *Be not drunken with wine, wherein is riot,*
> *but be filled with the Spirit ...*

Be filled with the Spirit. Now let me ask you, is your need emptiness? Yes, you're freed, but you're empty. Something's negative about you. You're delivered. There's not anything wrong, but there's a hollow feeling, an empty feeling. Something inside is not there. There's not that actual fullness.

Now, the Lord says be filled with the Spirit. Is your life spiritually aimless? The steering compunction of the Spirit of God is not there, so that you're just drifting from this meeting to that, from this saint to that, from this matter to that? What you need is to be filled. Are you empty?

Now look at this. It's rather wonderful. Note the exact wording. It says, "Be filled in the Spirit." Handley Moule has put it like this, "In the Holy Spirit, you can be filled." Now that's a wonderful thought. In the Holy Spirit, you can be filled. First you've got to be in the Holy Spirit, baptised in the Spirit. Then you can be filled. It's like a little cup being put in a bucket of water. Put the cup in the bucket of water and sink it and it's filled, absolutely filled to overflowing. I thought of a little poem that I came across some while ago by Amy Carmichael. Listen to it. I think it contains a wonderful thought.

Upon the sandy shore an empty shell,
Beyond the shell infinity of sea.
O Saviour, I am like that empty shell;
Thou art the sea to me.

A sweeping wave rides up the shore, and, lo,
Each dim recess the coiled shell within
Is searched, is filled, is filled to overflow
By water crystalline.

Not to the shell is any glory then:
All glory give we to the glorious sea
And not to me is any glory when
Thou overflowest me.

Sweep over me, Thy shell, as low I lie,
I yield me to the purpose of Thy will;
Sweep up, O conquering waves, and purify
And with Thy fulness fill.

She's just contained the thought we want to get over. We want to be like a shell submerged in the sea, in the infinity of the sea: filled to overflowing; filled to all the fullness of God. Now then, are you empty? Look at the context: "Speaking one to another in psalms and hymns and spiritual songs, singing and making melody with your heart." Instead of that dirge that comes out so often, that misery that spreads like an infection amongst all. "Oh, I've had such a terrible time."

The Lord said in this world we shall have tribulation. But He said, "Be of good cheer, I have overcome the world." Wouldn't it be wonderful if all of us were singing in our heart, making melody? What a wonderful thing. Then He goes on and it says, "Giving thanks always for all things in the name of our Lord Jesus Christ, to God, even the Father, subjecting yourselves one to another in the fear of the Lord."

How can you have all this wonderful praise, worship, thanksgiving, joy, peace and fellowship? By being filled with the Holy Spirit.

Now, look at the illustration in verse 18. "Be not drunk with wine." But what happens to a drunk person? The alcohol permeates every bit of their body. Every bit. It almost comes through their pores. It empowers them. It empowers them and controls them. "Be not drunk with wine, wherein is excess or riot, but be filled with the Spirit." Oh, to be permeated with the Spirit! You know, the first thing that attracted me about the present movement of the Spirit of God was some of the faces of the people who'd met the Lord. They were permeated with a radiancy. There were others that weren't, I must say that. But those that had a real experience were permeated with a radiancy. You could pick out the faces of people, because there was a peace, and there was a joy in the very face. There was something coming through the very pores of their being.

So it should be with us. "Be ye not drunk with wine, wherein is excess, but be filled with the Spirit." It doesn't mean that we're to lose control of ourselves and we're to fall all over the place, that we're to sort of start to behave as if we're mad. It means that somehow, the Holy Spirit within us can manifest the beauty of the Lord our God. So in us there is another agent other than ourselves.

Are You Powerless?

Now, that leads me to another scripture, Acts 1:8:

> *But ye shall receive power when the Holy*
> *Spirit is come upon you ...*

Now, can I ask you something? I've asked whether you feel naked. I've asked whether you feel empty. Now I want to ask you, do you feel weak? Paralysed? Dumb? Of course, there is a right kind of weakness. But God help us when it's the wrong kind of weakness. There is a weakness that makes us like a wet rag, that kind of droopy thing that no one can do anything with, just like a wet, foggy morning. Then people have got the cheek, and I mean it, the cheek to say, "When I am weak, then am I strong." What nonsense. What absolute nonsense.

The kind of weakness God speaks about is hidden in power. The kind of sorrow God speaks about is hidden in joy. The kind of conflict God speaks of is hidden in peace. Away with this kind of thing! If you wear it all on your arm, I should say that you're devoid of the Spirit of God, that's all. Paul said, "I can do all things through Christ who strengthens me. I have learned," he said, "in whatsoever state I am therewith to be content." He speaks of being abased and abounding. He speaks of finding the joy of the Lord there. He speaks of the peace of God which passes all understanding, garrisoning the heart and mind in Christ Jesus.

Now, I'm not saying that there are not times when we weep, and there are not times when we are down, and there are not times when we need to be lifted up and revived. But I am saying this: that the weakness that some people call weakness is wholly of the devil, wholly of the devil. It's something they've taken on from him and is not of God at all. Not at all. God doesn't expect you to go round in sort of greys, sombre, dark, like December 21st continually, instead of midsummer's day. The Lord wants you to be a person in whom He shines forth, someone in whom the life of His glory is seen. I have always discovered that the people who know what it is to be made weak are those whom many think are powerful. I've discovered that those with the greatest sorrows are the people that most think have no sorrows at all.

Some may say to these who seem sorrowless, "You don't understand us. You couldn't understand me." Sometimes I wonder if we want to, when I see some of the faces that come. No, all joking aside, the real point is that there is a weakness which is not of God. "Ye shall be clothed with power from on high. Ye shall receive power when the Holy Spirit is come upon you."

Are you dumb? Are you paralysed? Are you bound? Then the answer is this wonderful experience of the power of the Holy Spirit, the empowering of the Holy Spirit. Now, can I say one thing more about this verse, and we'll pass on to the last? It is this: you know, temperamentally and constitutionally, you and I will always remain the same, we will never be any different. After all, your personality is made up by what you are temperamentally. We don't all want to become little Pauls or little Peters. There is a Paul, and there is a Peter, and there is a John, and there's you and me, and there are others. We must remain temperamentally what we are and constitutionally what we are. Don't let's all try to copy each other temperamentally, as if our temperament is spiritual. It's not. The temperament is just the fragile vessel of clay, in many ways. The constitution is just part of the fragile vessel of clay, and will be in the glory, in a redemption body. But we shall have redemption bodies with temperaments.

Think of it: temperaments in the glory. Yes! Temperaments and constitutions, because we shall have redemption bodies. But, and this is the point, you can never make an excuse of your temperament and constitution. So many of us say, "Oh, well, that's me." So help us, God. It's a terrible thing just to simply say, "That's me." What you need is the power of the Holy Spirit that will transcend what you are temperamentally and constitutionally and balance you, and balance me, and fill out what we lack. You see, temperamentally we can be harsh, but the Holy Spirit can give us a grace. Temperamentally, we may be full of energy. The Holy Spirit can give us patience. It's not that we become different to what we are, but He balances us by indwelling us. There is a power which means that, instead of being tied to ourselves temperamentally and constitutionally, we rise above ourselves. We're not somehow, tied to what we are. Well, that's very important.

Are You Cold?

The last scriptures I want you to look at are Matthew 3:11, the last part:

> *... He shall baptise you in the Holy Spirit and in fire ...*

and in Acts 2:3. This is one that I know I've heard read so many times,

> *And there appeared unto them tongues parting asunder,*
> *like as of fire; and it sat upon each one of them.*

Have you ever thought about that? "There appeared tongues as of fire, parting asunder and dwelling on each one of them." Have you ever thought of the day of Pentecost? Of course, I suppose I first began to think about this in Austria, when I saw an old, old picture in the church of all these poor disciples (and I must say they looked very miserable) with a little flame of fire, each one, on the head and I thought, that's a strange picture. Then I thought, well, of course, it does say something about fire, doesn't it? So I went back and I looked. Of course, in a way, the artist has got it right. The fire came, and then it parted asunder and upon each one rested, abode, this fire.

Now, I want to ask you a question. Are you cold, spiritually? Oh, yes, you've got all the knowledge in the world. You know all about being crucified with Christ. You know what it is to have the indwelling of the Spirit. You even know something about the empowering of the Spirit up in your mind. But you're terribly cold. Loveless, cold, hard. Just like the Arctic. Are you like that spiritually? Well, I can soon give you a gauge.

Do you know what it is to worship? Can you really worship the Lord rapturously? I say it to myself, to every one of us. Can you? Can you really worship the Lord as if you love Him with your whole soul and heart? Don't say it's because you cannot do it in public. Nonsense. If you really love the Lord, and you knew He was here, you could be like that woman who broke that alabaster box. Do you remember there was a whole crowd of critical disciples gathered round murmuring? She was lost to the Lord, she couldn't care less about them all yapping in the background. She was worshipping the Lord.

It was like that other woman who once came and she wept at His feet and anointed Him. Again, a different woman, a woman who'd been saved. A woman of the streets. There was the host who sat by gathering his garments around him. The others, they were Pharisees who said, "How can this man be a holy man if he lets a woman like this touch him?" She was oblivious to them.

It says she went on bathing His feet with her tears while the Lord rebuked them. She was so oblivious to them. Don't tell me that you can't do it in public. I'll tell you what's wrong with you: you're not in love with the Lord. That's all.

Oh, you say, "I can't wear my heart on my sleeve." But your Lord wore His heart on His sleeve when He died on the cross for you. He was prepared to endure everything for you. He was prepared for all the taunting and the despising of everyone for you. I say it to my heart and to all our hearts. Are you cold? Well, here's the answer: "He shall baptise you in the Holy Spirit and in fire."

Fire, consumes. Fire consumes in a moment what is not of God. It will burn up in you what's not of God. Fire refines what is of God. It will purify, and refine, and develop. Fire lights. You know, our electricity comes from fire. The sun rises every day, and gives us light. You have the fire of the Spirit of God and there'll be light in your heart and light for other people. Your light will shine before men. There'll be warmth: fire warms us. There will be love in your heart: the love of God shed abroad in your heart by the Holy Spirit. Fire melts that hardness, that warpedness. Baptised in the fire, it will melt. It will absolutely melt. The thing in you that you never thought could ever change will just melt away because of the fire of God. Quickening.

The sun rises gradually, comes nearer to us in the spring, and draws out of the earth everything by its quickening power. So can fire do that with you. It can quicken you. Oh my, it can energise you. There's another little poem I'll share with you. It's by the woman who was such a tremendous blessing to brother Watchman Nee, and it's entitled *In the Wilderness for God*:

In the wilderness for God!
Just a common bush aflame!
Thus may I be, blessed Lord,
For the glory of Thy Name.

Just a common bush to be,
Something in which God can dwell,
Something thru which God can speak,
Something thru which God can tell,

All His yearning over men,
All His purposes of love,
Flaming with no light of earth,
But with glory from above:

God Himself within the bush,
Nothing seen but just the flame;
Make me that, just that, O God,
For the glory of Thy Name.

Margaret Barber wrote that. She was just like that—a dry old bush in China. She lived her whole life and saw very little for it. In the end, in the CMS (Church Missionary Society) when she came back, she said, "I'm not staying here. I'm going back." They said, "Well, we're not sending you back." So she said, "Well, I'll go back". She retired from the mission and went back, an old lady. She was just a dry old stick, nothing to look at. Nothing that you would have thought was unique or singular about Margaret Barber. She was just a common bush in the wilderness, but she was aflame for God. Watchman Nee caught light through Margaret Barber. It's not being sentimental to say that the whole core, spiritually, of China and perhaps of the world has been affected by one little old dry stick that you and I would have overlooked, but who was just a common bush aflame.

Appropriation By Faith

The necessity is appropriation by faith. Well, I ask you, do you need? God offers. That's all. God offers. Only three things can keep you back.

1. **Sin**—"If I regard iniquity in my heart, the Lord will not hear me."
2. **Ignorance**—Paul says, "Are ye ignorant?" If you're ignorant, that can keep you back.
3. **Unbelief**—"They fail to enter in through unbelief."

Only three things can hold you back from really experiencing the power and the indwelling of the Holy Spirit of God, bringing you into such an experience of the Lord that you're clothed, and filled, and empowered, and aflame. This could hold you back—that is if your eyes don't see what His nail-pierced hands offer you, and if you don't take this for yourself.

How to Receive God's Fire

Now, if you take, God will give. So confess, ask, receive, believe.

1. **Confess** your need.
2. **Ask** God exactly for what you need. Ask Him.

3. **Receive**. Open your heart. Say, "Lord Jesus, come. I take the Holy Spirit. I take that enduement with power from on high. I take the fullness tonight of the Spirit of God."
4. **Believe**. Thank the Lord. Thank Him, praise Him.

In His own time, He'll manifest it. There'll be a seal there. There'll be something for all to see, sealed with the Holy Spirit.

5.
Knowing the Holy Spirit as a Person

II Corinthians 3:4–8
And such confidence have we through Christ to God-ward: not that we are sufficient of ourselves, to account anything as from ourselves; but our sufficiency is from God; who also made us sufficient as ministers of a new covenant; not of the letter, but of the spirit: for the letter killeth, but the spirit giveth life. But if the ministration of death, written, and engraven on stones, came with glory, so that the children of Israel could not look steadfastly upon the face of Moses for the glory of his face; which glory was passing away: how shall not rather the ministration of the spirit be with glory?

II Corinthians 3:17–18
Now the Lord is the Spirit: and where the Spirit of the Lord is, there is liberty. But we all, with unveiled face beholding as in a mirror the glory of the Lord, are transformed into the same image from glory to glory, even as from the Lord the Spirit.

Shall we just bow together in a brief moment of prayer?

Father, we do want to thank Thee that we are here gathered in Thy presence, and that Thou hast made such glorious provision for us all to come before Thee joyfully and with confidence, to worship, to fellowship, to share what Thou hast given us of Thyself.

And, Lord, when we turn to Thy word, Thou hast made special provision, and we thank Thee for it, and we avail ourselves of that provision, for speaking and for hearing. We do thank Thee for all Thou art doing in the world. We pray, Lord, this day, that Thou gloriously own every single work of Thine with power and glory all through the earth, from the Far East to the Far West. We especially pray, Lord, for the Pope, and pray that thou wilt marvellously bless him on this visit to Poland, and thou wilt use him to the salvation of thousands of Polish people.

We thank Thee for the movement of Thy Spirit amongst Catholics in Poland and the Ukraine. Lord, we pray that Thou guard that visit from being manipulated by those who would use it for political reasons. But we pray, Lord, that Thou wilt grant that it shall end in the salvation of many precious souls.

O Lord, how amazing Thy works are. In these days, where we least expect Thee to be working, we find Thee working in power and with glory.

So, Lord, we give Thee thanks and we pray that we also may be involved in all that Thou art doing and be faithful to Thee till Thou shalt come. We ask it in the name of our Lord Jesus. Amen

The little verse that is much on my heart is this verse: II Corinthians 3:18.

> *But we all, with unveiled face beholding as in a mirror the glory of the Lord, are transformed into the same image from glory to glory, even as from the Lord the Spirit.*

What a wonderful, wonderful privilege it is to know the Holy Spirit. I suppose there is more controversy over the person and the work of the Holy Spirit at the present time than over any other matter. But I think it is tremendous to know the gracious and powerful ministry of the Holy Spirit.

I am sad when I notice people who, as soon as anything to do with the Holy Spirit is mentioned, you can almost see the shutters come down in their eyes and a kind of frozenness takes over within them. The devil has done his most insidious and subtle work in frightening people as to the person and work and power and gifts of the Holy Spirit. But here, in a nutshell, is the whole thing: "Now, the Lord is the Spirit, and where the Spirit of the Lord is, there is liberty."

What a statement. That, in itself, would be colossal enough and tremendous in its scope.

Bondage vs. True Freedom

"The Lord is the Spirit, and where the Spirit of the Lord is, there is liberty." Most Christians know bondage at some time or another in their experience and in their pilgrimage, and it is always because the Holy Spirit is quenched. Bondage always comes in the believer's life the moment the Holy Spirit is grieved or quenched in that life. Bondage always comes in a work of God whenever the Holy Spirit is grieved or quenched. Bondage always comes in an assembly, in the house of God, whenever the Holy Spirit is grieved or quenched. Do not think for one single moment that if we make a lot of noise, that is liberty and a sure sign that the Holy Spirit is present. It is no more an evidence that the Holy Spirit is present than are quietness and silence or a fear of interrupting.

Real liberty is to do the will of God from the heart. That is true freedom. To do the will of God, to walk in the way of God, even though you are fearful of the cost, even though you may be fearful of the unknown, of the possible consequences; to walk in in simple trust and faith in the way and will of God; *that* is true freedom.

True freedom is, when an issue comes up in our life or in our work, or in the house of God, you and I can die to ourselves. We are not bound to fight for our rights. We are not bound to defend ourselves. We are not bound to devalue the other person, the opponent, by one way or another. Real freedom is to lay down our lives for the Lord and for His people. Real freedom is to take the power and the gifts of the Holy Spirit. When a person is afraid, embarrassed, inhibited—there is a bondage.

Of course, it is perfectly right to say that on the matter of gifts, or the equipment of God, that it is more important to know the Lord Jesus in one sense than to exercise gifts. If you want to split theological hairs—of course it is more important to know the Lord Jesus, to love the Lord Jesus, to be devoted to the Lord Jesus, than to exercise gifts. But I do not see it as opposite, as some kind of matter to be placed one against the other.

Surely, if you love the Lord Jesus, you must find a way of meeting need. If you really love the Lord Jesus, you must find a way to be effective in testimony, in Christian work, in service, in prayer, in intercession and this requires the gifts and the equipment of God.

"The Lord is the Spirit and where the Spirit of the Lord is, there is freedom." Oh, such glorious freedom. Not just to bubble or to froth. Thank God when there is freedom even for that. We don't want to all be a kind of polite façade, all very correct, all very proper, all very nice, clean and sweetly dressed and so on. It is good when there is a freedom, so that we can all, even those who are a little less regular and a little less tidy, be able to express ourselves.

It is good. But these are things on the periphery. They are the superficialities. The real freedom that we want is the freedom to do the will of God; the freedom to be involved in the work of God; to see and to do the works of God. It is freedom, really, to lay down our lives for Him and freedom for His people. It is freedom to really take and appropriate all the power and the gifts and the equipment of the Holy Spirit, which we need if the purpose of God is to be fulfilled and realised.

With Unveiled Face

"We all with unveiled face." We sometimes think of the Jewish people as being those who have a veil over the heart. But I have to say that there is many a veil in a Christian heart. We are afraid to open up to God, afraid to investigate a matter objectively, impartially, afraid to really face the truth about things.

The word says, "we all with unveiled face." God's norm for the believer is to be unveiled. Nothing between, no need to put a veil on the face so that you do not see something fading, as Moses had to and is mentioned previously in the chapter. But ours is being changed from glory to glory.

Now I think we all have to say that most of us have experiences where the glow lasts with us for a while, but before long it begins to droop, it begins to fade. Isn't it so? I suppose most of us are guilty of Moses' answer to it, and that is to veil the face.

In other words, we project something one way or another. But the apostle, by the Spirit says, we don't want to have any veils, we don't want to have any façades, we don't want to have any fading glory. "But we all with unveiled face beholding as in a mirror, the glory of the Lord, are changed into the same image from glory to glory, even as from the Lord, the Spirit"—changed into the same image.

How we behold the glory of the Lord is in a mirror. These mirrors were metal mirrors, not the kind of mirrors we have today where we get a pretty exact image of ourselves. We may not always like what we see in there, but we see something pretty exact. But this mirror that the apostle speaks of is the kind of metal mirror, and this did not give an exact image.

This is how we see the glory of the Lord. We do not yet see face to face. If anyone has ever been ravished by what they have seen of the Lord—if you have ever been in an ecstasy over what the Lord has revealed to you of Himself, if any of you have almost ever been transported out of your bodies by some touch from God—what will it be when we see Him face to face?

No wonder the old saints called it the *rapture*, to be enraptured; when we are raptured face to face to see the Lord for the first time, not as in a mirror, darkly or dimly or approximately, but absolutely, directly? How marvellous it is going to be.

But what a privilege is ours now to behold the glory of the Lord as in a mirror—“beholding as in a mirror the glory of the Lord.”

Conformed to the Image of the Son

As we behold the Lord, the glory of the Lord, we see the beauty of the Lord, the fullness of the Lord, we are changed into the same image, from glory to glory. You know, in the end, it is not your zeal that is the lasting value. It is not your knowledge of the Bible or your knowledge of spiritual things or even your knowledge of the ways of God culled from past experience. That is not the lasting value. The lasting value of your life is how much you have been changed into the image of the Lord Jesus.

That is the eternal value of your life. It is what marks you out from all other human beings not saved by the grace of God. You are to be changed, conformed to the image of God’s own Son. This work is not something that just happens in the twinkling of an eye. You can be a difficult, hypocritical, crab-like believer and suddenly the Lord comes and in the twinkling of an eye you become a fully-fledged, mature, beautiful saint? I don’t find that in the Book. It seems to me that, in this short span of time, we have to allow the Lord to do a work in our lives that will change us from glory to glory.

Now, who does this work? The actual person who does the work is not the Father, nor the Son, but the Holy Spirit. You cannot contradict me on that because it is here clearly stated in the Book.

Apart from the person of the Holy Spirit, you cannot come to the Lord. You cannot be born of God. You cannot come into union with God in Christ. You cannot know what it is to be equipped for service. You cannot be changed into the same image.

Controversy Over the Holy Spirit

Now, there has been all sorts of controversy in our day over the Holy Spirit's baptism: His coming upon people, His empowering them, His gifting them. It seems it is quite all right if you are filled with the Holy Spirit, but should you dare to speak in a tongue, this is devilish. If you should open your mouth and prophesy, this is something essentially erroneous and false.

There are those who tell us that all this went out at the beginning of the church era, with the completion of the canon. But we see in fact that, again and again, most embarrassingly, it has reappeared in church history.

In fact, if we are to say that it is all demonic, devilish and satanic, we cut out whole portions of the Christian church. The Anabaptists, some of the earlier reformers, the early Methodists, the Quakers. Oh dear, we go back earlier to Albigenses, Waldenses, Bogomils, Priscillianists, even the Huguenots. It is embarrassing the amount of evidence that we see all through church history. Yet some seem to be, by and large, very much against the charismatic movement. I cannot understand it.

The evidence of church history is that these gifts of the Holy Spirit, this equipment of God, has never disappeared. In fact, whenever the Holy Spirit has moved again in fresh ways, there has been a manifestation.

Coming Upon vs. Coming Into

What interests me is that all the fuss is about the Holy Spirit coming upon people. In actual fact, this was the experience of God's people all through the Old Testament. The Holy Spirit was always coming upon people. Why, even Saul, in all his fleshliness, prophesied, and all those who were with them—you remember, they fell on the ground and prophesied for about 24 hours. My goodness, even Balaam's ass prophesied when the Holy Spirit touched her!

The whole of the Old Covenant is full of the Holy Spirit coming upon people. The early church never had any problem about the Holy Spirit coming upon people. Their great excitement was that the Holy Spirit had come not *upon* them, but *into* them.

This was the fulfilment of the words of Jeremiah the prophet in the wonderful words of Jeremiah 31:33–34.

> *But this is the covenant that I will make with the house of Israel after those days, saith the Lord: I will put my law in their inward parts, and in their heart will I write it; and I will be their God, and they shall be my people. And they shall teach no more every man his neighbour, and every man his brother, saying, Know the Lord; for they shall all know me, from the least of them unto the greatest of them, saith the Lord: for I will forgive their iniquity, and their sin will I remember no more.*

Isn't it marvellous? And when we take with that the words of the prophet Ezekiel, which we find in Ezekiel 36:26–27:

> *A new heart also will I give you, and a new spirit will I put within you; and I will take away the stony heart out of your flesh, and I will give you a heart of flesh. And I will put my Spirit within you, and cause you to walk in my statutes, and ye shall keep mine ordinances, and do them.*

Here is the wonder of this new covenant: not only does the Holy Spirit come upon us, over which there is so much controversy today, but the Holy Spirit comes *within* us. Now, in one sense, we cannot surgically divide the indwelling of the Holy Spirit from the empowering of the Holy Spirit. It is perfectly true that the Holy Spirit takes up residence within us when we are born again, by the coming upon us of the Holy Spirit. This is as necessary as the indwelling of the Holy Spirit.

What we need to experience and know is the fullness of the work of the Holy Spirit. I imagine there is hardly anybody who would disagree with what I have said. But what I want to underline is this, because I believe it is the missing key in this whole matter of the work of the Holy Spirit: Christians have developed a tragic and fatal mistake—a tendency to look upon the Holy Spirit as a *thing*, as an *it*, as a *power*, as an *equipment*, as *gifts*, and not realise that the Holy Spirit is the third person of the Godhead.

It is this which is the key that unlocks everything.

Knowing the Spirit as a Person

You see, I have come to know the Father, and I find one of the most wonderful things in the world is to know *our Father who is in heaven*; to know the Spirit of God shed abroad in my heart, crying "Abba, Father." It is wonderful to get to know God as Father, isn't it? To know the fatherhood of God, the care of God, the love of God, the safety and security which stems from His fatherhood? It is wonderful to be a child of God.

Of course, we hardly need to say anything about the Lord Jesus and knowing the Lord Jesus. For so many of us, it was this that captured our whole heart: the centrality of the Lord Jesus. To know Him!

We have found so many Christians who when they were converted, did not *know* the Lord. They knew Him simply as Saviour. But they did not know Him as someone they could really talk to intimately, getting to know Him. It is wonderful to know the Lord Jesus.

Now, the Holy Spirit does not speak of Himself. He is always drawing our attention to the Father and to the Son. But this does not mean that the Holy Spirit is not the person of the Holy Spirit. You and I have to get to know the person of the Holy Spirit, the third person of the Godhead, as intimately as we know the Father and the Son. Here there is something so wonderful. Listen again to the apostle's words he says in this II Corinthians 3:17–18.

> *Now the Lord is the Spirit: and where the Spirit of the Lord is, there is liberty. But we all, with unveiled face beholding as in a mirror the glory of the Lord, are transformed into the same image from glory to glory, even as from the Lord the Spirit.*

There could not be anything clearer, could there? *The Lord, the Spirit.*

I think that there is, in many of our hearts and lives, an area of ignorance. We have not known the Holy Spirit—as the Lord, the Spirit—but only as the *means* by which God does a work in us; the means by which we are brought to God; the means by which we know repentance, or new birth, or union. We have known Him as some kind of powerful energy that enables us to do a job. No wonder the Holy Spirit is grieved. No wonder, sometimes, the Holy Spirit is quenched.

Some people seem to think that under the New Covenant, all that God does has no connection with time. But God respects seasons and times. It is interesting that, when Jesus died, He died on Passover. There could have been nothing more glorious and more wonderful than that the Lamb of God should have died at about the time the lambs were being sacrificed in the temple in readiness for the Passover. There could not have been anything more wonderful!

The Holy Spirit came on the feast that is called, in the Old Covenant, the Feast of Weeks. In Hebrew, *Shavuot*—the Feast of Weeks. What is the Feast of Weeks? Two marvellous things: first, it commemorates the giving of the law by God to the children of Israel through Moses. Secondly, it is the Festival of First Fruits. It is the first figs, the first apricots, the first almonds; the first of everything is in the market.

Don't you think it is marvellous that the Holy Spirit should come on this festival, surely with meaning? Before, the law came dead, it says in II Corinthians 3, *engraven* on stone. It came with glory, although it was the dead letter, and it drove us like a schoolmaster to Christ. The Holy Spirit came to bring that law from without to within and write it on our hearts and give us the energy and the power to do the will of God and keep the word of God, the law of God, from within.

"I will write My law upon their hearts. I will put My Spirit within them." I find that wonderful. And first fruits? Well, I do not know how you feel about fruit, whether you feel there is a little bit of fruit in your life; if there is, it is the work of the Holy Spirit.

Seeking the Person of the Holy Spirit

What then can we say to anybody who feels that, somehow or other, there is an area of ignorance in their life? Such a person would say, "You know, I have heard about the Holy Spirit. I know about the person of the Holy Spirit. It has not come to us as revelation, but we accept it. But, somehow or other, there is an area of ignorance. I do not feel that I have yet broken the spiritual sound barrier over the matter of the Holy Spirit." I would not tell you, "Go away and seek an experience." What I would say is, "Go away and ask God from this day to begin to reveal to you the person of the Holy Spirit."

Don't just make it a one moment prayer. Begin consistently to seek the Lord as to the person of the Holy Spirit. Ask the Holy Spirit to come to you. Tell Him that you do not want to grieve Him; you do not want to quench Him. You know that He means everything in the work of God. It was, after all, through the Holy Spirit that the formless void and chaos of the world came into the creation and it was through the Holy Spirit that even the Son of God was formed in the womb of the virgin Mary. And it was through the Spirit of God that Jesus did all the mighty works of

God, for He calls it, in Luke 11:20, by the *finger of God*, a term for the Holy Spirit.

It was by the eternal Spirit that He offered Himself up on the cross without spot or blemish unto God. It was that Spirit of Him who raised up Jesus from the dead that is to dwell in you and in me. Oh, if we would only go back to God and start to seek Him about this! If we would say, "I want to be honest. I want to know You, Holy Spirit. I want to know You in my own experience. I want not error, not counterfeit, not falsity, not façade. I want to know You."

In the way that the Spirit brought you to Jesus, the Lord Jesus will bring you to the Holy Spirit. He will take you, and He will immerse you in the person of God, the Spirit.

Shall we pray?

Father, Thou knowest all our hearts and lives. They are an open book to Thee, Lord. There is nothing hid from Thee. We all want to be honest, Lord, and sincere and real and we all feel, or at least many of us feel, Lord, an area in our lives of ignorance when it comes to the real work of the Holy Spirit. We are saved, Lord. We know that we are born of Thy Spirit—we know that. We are, Lord, in union with Thee with the measure—we know that. But, Lord, we feel that there is some breakthrough in many of our lives where we just need to come to know the blessed Holy Spirit. We pray in the name of Jesus on this day when we commemorate that coming of Thyself upon that hundred and twenty. We want to ask Thee, Holy Spirit, touch us.

Touch us, Lord.

Oh, dear Lord Jesus, immerse us in the person of the Holy Spirit. May all our reserve or caution or bondage disappear because the

Spirit of the Lord comes upon us and takes up, in a new way, residence within us.

Dear Lord, we commit ourselves to Thee. We pray that Thou wilt watch over Thy word. Do not let it be lost, Lord, we pray. Do not let some desire in our hearts, some challenge that may have come to us to which we have responded, be lost in the welter of routine life. But we pray, Lord, that in some way Thou wilt help us to respond to Thee and to go through with Thee on this matter. We ask it together in the name of our Lord Jesus.

Amen.

6.
The Outpouring of the Holy Spirit

Joel 2:28–32

And it shall come to pass afterward, that I will pour out my Spirit upon all flesh; and your sons and your daughters shall prophesy, your old men shall dream dreams, your young men shall see visions: and also upon the servants and upon the handmaids in those days will I pour out my Spirit. And I will show wonders in the heavens and in the earth: blood, and fire, and pillars of smoke. The sun shall be turned into darkness, and the moon into blood, before the great and terrible day of the Lord cometh. And it shall come to pass, that whosoever shall call on the name of the Lord shall be delivered; for in mount Zion and in Jerusalem there shall be those that escape, as the Lord hath said, and among the remnant those whom the Lord doth call.

I would like to begin with a reminder that these prophecies of Joel have a dual fulfilment. What I mean by this is that they have a first fulfilment, and they have also a second fulfilment. It is quite clear from the way that they have been given to us and the way, in fact, that the New Testament uses them, that the prophecy of Joel, particularly in Joel 2:28–32, has not been exhausted, but has been given to us to describe the age in which we now are all found: the age, if you like, of the Holy Spirit.

The Holy Spirit is the very character of this age: He is the one who began it; He is the one who watches over its progress; and He is the one who is going to complete it. In a peculiar way, the Holy Spirit is bound up to this age, this New Testament age. It seems to me, if we consider the prophecies of Joel, that in the days in which we live, nothing less nor anything more than a counterpart to Pentecost could possibly, finally realise God's original purpose and bring back the Lord Jesus Christ at the end of this age.

When you look at world conditions and see the impossibility of everything, it is clearly evidenced already that the conditions and the energy which is opposed to us is far, far too great for all the ingenuity of Christians combined.

In a sense, it is true that wherever there has been a need of a supernatural deliverance, there has been a supernatural provision.

Supernatural Deliverance and Supernatural Provision

God had to deliver a people from Egypt. It was far too much for the combined ingenuity of His children in Egypt, they could have had a thousand Moseses, and they still could not have got themselves out of Egypt. They could have had all the thousands and thousands of God's people with one heart and with one soul and with one mind, really wanting the Lord and wanting His way. But still, it needed a supernatural deliverance. The Passover was something supernatural. The Exodus was a supernatural deliverance. It was the birth of the people of God as a nation. The Jewish people still trace the inception of their nationality, their nationhood, back to the Passover and the Exodus. You see, it was a supernatural deliverance that was needed, so supernatural provision was made. There was a pillar of cloud and fire which led them. The angel of the Lord went before them, and behind them there was the manna that was brought down from heaven, the water that was brought out of the rock. There was that which was obviously beyond man. What was impossible by human standards was gloriously possible by the Holy Spirit.

Now it has been so that, in church history, again and again God's people have had to face an overwhelming alliance of evil. When you look back into church history, you will discover again and again that every real move in this world, as far as even social revolution goes, can be traced back in so many instances to a primary moving and outpouring of the Holy Spirit. In England, for instance, most social reform can be traced back almost directly to the outpouring of the Holy Spirit in preceding generations. Take just a few things, such as the child reform bill that was passed through Parliament around the turn of the twentieth century as a direct result of the Second Great Evangelical Awakening. Going back even further you find that prison reform was a direct result of the Quaker movement, and further back beyond that were many other reforms. We could go on and on about these things—but that is not our point.

We are simply saying this: that whenever the church has

been decadent, and whenever it has been powerless, whenever it has been just a thing of derision and scorn in the eyes of the multitudes, the only thing that has recovered the true nature of this church and enthroned the Lord Jesus again in a new way has been an outpouring of the Holy Spirit.

We are by nature so narrow, so prejudiced, so immovable, or on the other hand, so sentimental and so wishy-washy that we need the Holy Spirit in a new way to take hold of us and meet the situation. When you look at the prophet Joel, he seems to hold out for us a hope as he describes what it will be like toward the latter part of the New Testament age, as he describes something of the powers that will be against God's people, as he describes the absolute decadence of the church and the moral collapse of the nations. As he describes all these things, he sets forth one answer: that the Lord Himself will pour out His Spirit on all flesh, so that there shall be, if only in a remnant, an answer to the terrible situation and to the downward trend of the world.

Now, if you look at Isaiah, you will find he says exactly the same. He sees it from a slightly different point of view, but it is the same message that he has. If you look at Isaiah 61, you will find the great declaration of the Lord Himself. In Isaiah 61:1, we read this:

> *The Spirit of the Lord Jehovah is upon me; because Jehovah hath anointed me to preach good tidings unto the meek*

Now, if you will look in the gospel, you will find the Lord Jesus quoted this as being fulfilled in Himself. The prophet Isaiah was speaking of the Lord Jesus, the one upon whom was the Spirit of the Lord God, who had been anointed to a great ministry and task which He accomplished. Therefore, when you come to chapter 61, you find it is the Lord speaking. It is not Isaiah, the prophet, who is speaking. It is not the church who is speaking. It is the Lord Himself who is speaking and what is the burden of the Lord's heart?

If you read from Isaiah 40, forgetting the chapter divisions and the verse divisions, just reading it right through, what will you come to see? You find a tremendous setting forth, in a logical sequence, of the work of the Lord Jesus, beginning with John the Baptist, the Elijah who went before Him, saying, "Prepare ye. Prepare ye a way for the Lord," then going right on to the Lord Jesus and His ministry and that tremendous chapter, Isaiah 53: His death, His crucifixion. Then, immediately when you come to chapter 54, you are in a new atmosphere. For the first time, the person has given way to a family.

One has become a nation. Immediately, it speaks of a family enlargement on every side. As you go through, you begin to read of the great battle that there is going to be over this family. If the devil could not stop the Lord Jesus' work, if he could not stop the testimony of the Lord Jesus personally, if he could not stop the work being finished on the cross, then the devil was going to combine all his forces to destroy what we call the church.

If he cannot destroy Jesus, he will try to destroy the church.

The Embattled Church

Church history is the very exemplification of that statement. It is the long and bloody story of man's cruelty to Christian people.

Everywhere, in every generation, in every century, Christians have been hounded to their death. This very hour, there are Christians who are dying in this world. In this century, with all its social advancement and education and so-called culture, there are Christians dying for nothing else than their faith in the Lord Jesus Christ.

What is it? It is the devil's hatred of what is called, in Scripture, *Zion*. The devil hates it. Of course—he hates Christ. If we look at our New Testament, we will discover that the church is none other than a corporate Christ; that is all. That is why the devil hates the church.

The church consists of the very members of Christ. It is the body of Christ. It is so united to Christ, so part of Christ, so essentially part of His very being that the Bible reveals it to us as Christ. The church is Christ.

Ephesians 1:23 says of the church that "it is the fullness of Him that filleth all in all." The devil says, "I cannot get to the Head. He is in the glory. The Head is at the right hand of God. I cannot touch Him, I cannot destroy Him, but I can destroy His members. I can get at the members; I can get at His body, and I can mutilate it, and devour it, and hound it, and persecute it, and break it, if it is at all possible."

You will find throughout church history, again and again, these slow, insidious, subtle buildups of satanic alliance, and then a swooping down on them.

Think of that tremendous, move of the Holy Spirit in Bohemia, when over two-thirds of the Bohemian people were converted within a few years to the Lord Jesus Christ. Such a movement of the Spirit has not been seen in Europe for many centuries. But, in one night, 36,000 of those people were massacred—36,000 in one night. Think of that great move, which was a church move. All these things I am talking about, were not just religious movements. I am talking about church moves, in their beginnings. Whatever they became later is another thing, but at the beginning ...!

Take that great move that we call the Huguenot movement. How tremendous that was. But, in one night, thousands upon thousands upon thousands were murdered. What is this? What is it? I do not think it is man. Behind man, there is some vile satanic power that is out, at all costs, by one means or another, to destroy what we call the church.

So, when you come here to the Lord Jesus, what is the burden of the Lord's heart? Why, read Isaiah 62:1:

> *For Zion's sake will I not hold my peace, and for Jerusalem's sake I will not rest, until her righteousness go forth as brightness, and her salvation as a lamp that burneth.*

I remember once speaking with a dear brother about this matter, and I remember one little thing that he said to me (and he had studied church history). He said to me, "You know, it seems to me that there has been a kind of system in church history whereby first, you have an outpouring of the Holy Spirit; then, a great move in the right direction; and then a terrible satanic blow whereby the whole thing has been ruined and then it just becomes some dead thing. But, in every generation, you have got the same result."

Well, of course, today we are living in it. In China, for example, there was a tremendous move during the first half of the twentieth century that covered the whole nation from end to end and now the thing has been ruined.

For Zion's Sake—An Eternal Building

Obliterated. Thousands have given their lives for the Lord Jesus Christ. Why is this allowed? Because, you see, it is all going *up*. That is why. God can dare to allow such things, because it is something eternal that He is building. So long as we are in the purpose of God down here, and so long as is possible, as long as we are moving in what we could call a church move of the Holy Spirit, then let the devil destroy us.

What has been wrought down here goes up there. That is the point. What comes out down here is the material for the city. That is the point! The material for the city doesn't just materialise out of heaven. It comes out of heaven. Thank God, it comes out of heaven. But the material came up from earth. Oh, yes. The material, if you read, was in the garden of Eden, right down in the earth. It has got to be taken out, it has got to be worked upon, and then it is sent up. Finally, one day, you will see it coming.

But where is all this? Well, it is in Zion.

Zion is what the Lord is after. On the one side, we must not be afraid of all the trouble and trial and problem and breakdown and failure down here that we are bound to get. So long as we are on what we call church ground, so long as we are on that ground upon which God can really build us together and get on with the job, let us get on with it. Every time Satan has really attacked His people, it has been because there has been a church move. That is all. If anyone is disposed to argue with me, look back into church history. You will come to the same conclusion.

Every single thing that we now know today as a denomination began as a church move; began as a move of the Holy Spirit in the right direction. In its day and generation, it was the testimony. In its day and generation, it began with a pouring out of the Holy Spirit. Then, slowly, insidiously, by frontal attack or from within, Satan has gradually veered the thing off and got it out of the way as well.

We do not persecute people who don't count.

No need to do anything. We can let them preach, let them work, let them have their organisation of activity, everything else, just carry on. Satan does not mind that much. If he cannot stop people being saved, he is going to stop them being built up. If he cannot stop the Lord Jesus seeing the travail of His soul in people actually being saved, then the next thing he will stop is the church. He will stop those people being built together down here and so, in the end, becoming part of the city up there.

When you read Isaiah 62, you will find the burden of the Lord's heart. It is for Zion. He is not going to rest. He will have no peace. Why? "Until her righteousness go forth as brightness and her salvation as a lamp that burneth." Isn't that wonderful?

You and I are so weak in prayer. Why don't we take the Scripture and stand on it and ask the Lord to do something about it? The Lord said it Himself, after the cross, after Pentecost. If you look through this wonderful prophecy of Isaiah, Jesus says: now My continual intercession at the Father's right hand is going to be about Zion. I am not going to rest. I am going to intercede day and night for Zion. Do you not think the Lord knows better than

I the condition of His church? Do you think that He knows if it is decadent, if it has collapsed, if it is powerless, if it is superficial? Doesn't the Lord know better than we? Is not the burden of His intercessory ministry for His Zion, that something will happen to it? I think so. I believe so, and what is the burden of His prayer? He will not rest until her salvation goes forth as a lamp that burneth. That is the testimony. That is the lampstand. He is not going to rest until it is back.

Oh, dear, brothers and sisters, we have seen in church history, in every generation, a move of the Holy Spirit. If we believe that we are approaching the end of the age, should we not pray? Oh, Lord, Lord, make Zion as a lamp. Give Zion a salvation that goes forth as a lamp that burneth. Should we not make this our prayer? Should not the Lord's own word be the basis of our prayer? Why is our prayer so weak? It is because we have not got the basis for it. It is all conjecture, all speculation. "Lord, could you bless so-and-so? Lord, bless something else over there. Lord, do something here." Then we wonder "Now, have I prayed according to the will of God? Is that in the Spirit of God? Is that according to what He wants?"

You and I have the word of God upon which we can settle and we can say, "Lord, this is your burden. Now then, we are going to pray like this." We are going to pray and that is exactly—if you read on in Isaiah 62, it is exactly what Isaiah says. The Lord says, "Now, Zion, I have set watchmen upon thy walls." You must take no rest and you must give Him no rest until He does it.

Oh, for an intercessory prayer ministry like that! Do you honestly think that more activity, more organisation, more money, more manpower is going to counteract the situation in the church today, or is going to counteract the world in general? Do you? I don't think so. It needs a pouring out of the Holy Spirit in a new way that will be upon all Christians; not just us, not those that we love to say, "who have seen," but upon *all*, that will just break open their eyes so that they suddenly say, "I see something I've never seen before."

Believe me, many of us are prejudiced. We need the Holy Spirit. We think we are unprejudiced, untraditional, and everything else, but we have got the same old earthly mould which slowly puts its clammy hands upon us and before we know it, and whilst we are unconscious of it, we have become some other thing. We think along certain rigid and frigid lines.

The Burden of the Holy Spirit

We need the Holy Spirit. The Holy Spirit is the most wonderful person of all because He's always doing things that turn us upside-down. You say, "Ah, now, now, the Holy Spirit can't do that" and immediately He does it, and then you sit down and think, "Oh dear, oh dear, dear, dear." Then people have to say, "Well, it can't be the Lord. It can't be the Lord Jesus. He has done something that we have always said was wrong." But no, you see, the Holy Spirit is sovereign.

You and I cannot tell the Holy Spirit what to do. The Holy Spirit, when He comes in a new way, so opens us up that we become bound to the Lord Jesus in a new way and are prepared to follow the Lamb withersoever He goeth. I am afraid that so often we have such theological conceptions that, if the Lamb were to go *that* way, we could not go. We would say, "No, no, no, I can't do it."

But you see, the way that the Lord has of doing something which we have seen is often altogether different from the way we think He will do it.

What the Lord wants and sees as His objective and what you and I see as His objective may be absolutely one. We may all be seeing the same objective, but it is the way the Lord is going to get to His objective and the way you and I *think* the Lord is going to get to His objective which is all the trouble.

We need the Holy Spirit to break us wide open and make us a people who can just follow the Lamb and say, "Well, Lord, we can't understand it. You have dealt by the cross without prejudice with so much else. We just have to follow you. But we don't understand it. But we are sure you are going this way."

Oh, for a ministry of prayer like that in the book of Acts. Well, some of you may say, "Oh, he has got a bee in the bonnet now about Pentecost and other things such as that. I think he is reading into Isaiah what really is not in Isaiah." But I would like to point you to this: read through chapter 63 of Isaiah, and you will discover in chapter 63 that it is all about the collapse of God's people. They have become a reproach. They have become a despising. Similarly in our day the nations are saying, "Oh, the church." Oh, how many times I have heard that in this town of Richmond and the young people, whenever you say the church … "The *church*." They spit it out: "the *church*." A term of derision. In Isaiah 63, you will find exactly what Isaiah describes: God's people have become a derision, a reproach, a butt for jokes. Something with no authority and no real, inward, moral, spiritual power.

Then what is Isaiah's cry? I believe Isaiah understood. "Oh," he says in chapter 64, "Oh, that Thou wouldst rend the heavens, that

Thou wouldst come down, that the mountains might flow down at Thy presence," and so on. You see, he had got it. This was the Holy Spirit that was needed to just simply cause the mountains in us and outside of us just to flow down.

If you read verse seven of chapter 64, you will find Isaiah's heartbreak is that there is "none that calleth upon Thy name that stirreth up himself to take hold of Thee, for Thou hast hid Thy face from us."

Well, there you are. Read right through to chapter 65 and on and you will find that the end is a glorious end. The end is, in fact, what we sometimes call the millennium. It is the reign of Christ, when "the wolf shall dwell with the lamb, and the leopard shall lie down with the kid; and the calf and the young lion and the fatling together" and so on.

You see? Christ has come back.

The end of Isaiah's prophecy is: the Lord comes. Not only is the Holy Spirit given and Zion is put into her rightful place and the nations of the world come to Zion, but the Lord returns and His reign of peace begins.

I am not the least bit bothered if the Lord's return is still a thousand years off. The point is this: we are living in conditions that are decadent, immoral and show on every side collapse of personal integrity.

It is everywhere.

There are great moves afoot in the nations, things that may have tremendous repercussions and consequences that few of us realise now. Where are we as God's people? We are nowhere! Even if the Lord's return is a thousand years ahead (the most conservative estimate), I must say that we still need the Holy

Spirit in *our* day and in *our* generation to do something that will make Zion's salvation go forth as a lamp that burns. I believe it is very important and it needs, by the Holy Spirit, to get into our hearts so that we have a basis for prayer.

The Revealed Will of God

Every prayer that has been answered in Scripture has been based upon the revealed will of God. We have here, within the very Scriptures, not a little scriptural textbook, or a collection of verses that you pick out to get a little comfort for now and again. Maybe it is used in that way with blessing, but that is not the use of scriptures primarily. It is to give to us God's whole scheme of things. What God is after, what He is wanting to do, and everything else—you will find it all here. If we were more practical in our approach to the Bible, why, everything would be revolutionised and I believe we have here, within the Scriptures, the revealed will of God in any given situation.

We have a situation, an international situation, which needs the intercessory, relentless prayer of God's people to do something in His Zion. If God would do something in His Zion, He could do something in the nations. Every single person who wanted to come to the Lord could come to the Lord, if only we put first things first. I am not depreciating the work of missions and so much of missionary activity. Thank God for it all! But the whole point is that what we need is a new move of the Holy Spirit that will cause the Lord to be expressed in His body in a new way worldwide.

The end of that may be a crucifixion for all who take part in it, but the material will be there, and the material will go up, and it will bring back the King.

May the Lord Jesus Christ help us very greatly to see the significance and importance of what we have said.

7. The Recovery of the Church and the Holy Spirit

Joel 2:28–32

And it shall come to pass afterward, that I will pour out my Spirit upon all flesh; and your sons and your daughters shall prophesy, your old men shall dream dreams, your young men shall see visions: and also upon the servants and upon the handmaids in those days will I pour out my Spirit. And I will show wonders in the heavens and in the earth: blood, and fire, and pillars of smoke. The sun shall be turned into darkness, and the moon into blood, before the great and terrible day of the Lord cometh. And it shall come to pass, that whosoever shall call on the name of the Lord shall be delivered; for in mount Zion and in Jerusalem there shall be those that escape, as the Lord hath said, and among the remnant those whom the Lord doth call.

Ezekiel 37:1–14

The hand of the Lord was upon me, and he brought me out in the Spirit of the Lord, and set me down in the midst of the valley; and it was full of bones. And he caused me to pass by them round about: and, behold, there were very many in the open valley; and, lo, they were very dry. And he said unto me, Son of man, can these bones live? And I answered, O Lord Jehovah, thou knowest. Again he said unto me, Prophesy over these bones, and say unto them, O ye dry bones, hear the word of the Lord. Thus saith the Lord Jehovah unto these bones: Behold, I will cause breath to enter into you, and ye shall live. And I will lay sinews upon you, and will bring up flesh upon you, and cover you with skin, and put breath in you, and ye shall live; and ye shall know that I am the Lord.

So I prophesied as I was commanded: and as I prophesied, there was a noise, and, behold, an earthquake; and the bones came together, bone to its bone. And I beheld, and, lo, there were sinews upon them, and flesh came up, and skin covered them above; but there was no breath in them. Then said he unto me, Prophesy unto the wind [or to the Spirit], *prophesy, son of man, and say to the wind, Thus saith the Lord Jehovah: Come from the four winds, O breath, and breathe upon these slain, that they may live. So I prophesied as he commanded me, and the breath came into them, and they lived, and stood up upon their feet, an exceeding great army.*

Then he said unto me, Son of man, these bones are the whole house of Israel: behold, they say, Our bones are dried up, and our hope is lost; we are clean cut off. Therefore prophesy, and say unto them, Thus saith the Lord Jehovah: Behold, I will open your graves, and cause you to come up out of your graves, O my people; and I will bring you into the land of Israel. And ye shall know that I am the Lord, when I have opened your graves, and caused you to come up out of your graves, O my people. And I will put my Spirit in you, and ye shall live, and I will place you in your own land: and ye shall know that I, the Lord, have spoken it and performed it, saith the Lord.

There is a book that has always been a great blessing to me, and I expect it has also been the same to many others. That book is *The Pilgrim Church*, by E.H. Broadbent. I think it is one of the finest accounts of church history written, and certainly one of the soundest.

I think it would be very good for us to hear the conclusions that are found at the end of this book, written in the early part of the twentieth century. E.H. Broadbent was a very great and godly man, who was used very much of the Lord in Russia and in Eastern Europe. His account of church history is accepted now by Christians of all different thoughts and viewpoints as a standard work.

So, I would like first to hear what Broadbent has to say at the end of his history, and then I am going to make some final observations concerning the prophet Jonah and the prophet Joel. Now, it may not be to everyone's liking, so I might just say right now that if you feel that this dear brother is critical, I suggest you read the whole book first before you criticise his conclusions.

After all, his conclusions are based upon the other 17 chapters of this volume.[1]

> The church question, that is to say, the question whether we can, and should, continue to carry out the New Testament teaching and example as to the ordering of churches, has been answered in various ways.
>
> [There is, firstly,] the theory of "development" which would make it undesirable to do so, because, as is claimed by the ritualistic churches such as the Church of Rome, the Greek Orthodox Church, and others like them, something better than that which was practised in the beginning, in the New Testament, has been attained, and the Scriptures have been modified or even supplanted by tradition.
>
> Secondly, Rationalism gives the same answer, looking upon it as retrogression to go back to the original pattern, since it denies that the Scriptures provide an abiding authority.
>
> Thirdly, the reformers of existing churches have tried to effect a compromise, returning in part, but not altogether, to the acknowledged pattern, as Luther, Spener, and others.
>
> Fourthly, some have abandoned the attempt, as the Mystics, who devoted themselves instead to the attainment of personal holiness and communion with God, examples of whom are Molinos and Madame Guyon, Tersteegen, and the Friends, who set aside the outward ordinances of baptism and the Lord's Supper, and occupied themselves rather with the testimony of the inner Light than with the outward scriptures;

1 The following is an excerpt from E.H. Broadbent's *The Pilgrim Church*. The text in brackets shows Lance's words rather than Broadbent's

others, as Darby and his followers, repudiated the obligation and replaced it by a witness to "the ruin of the Church."

Fifthly, evangelical revival set it aside as unimportant, concentrating on the conversion of sinners and organising what seemed suitable to meet practical needs, as Wesley's Methodist Societies or the Salvation Army.

Or sixthly, but there have in all times been brethren who have answered "yes" to the question, though they have been called by many names: Cathars, Novatians, Paulicians, Bogomils, Albigenses, Waldenses, Lollards, Anabaptists, Mennonites, Stundists, and others innumerable, many congregations also are Baptists and Independents, and assemblies of Brethren; they have been one [in the different centuries] in their endeavor to act upon the New Testament and to follow the example of the New Testament churches.

Closely connected with the former question is another: Is it possible today to preach the gospel as at the beginning, and might not a much more rapid spread of the gospel result from so doing? Indeed, the question enlarges and presses itself upon us: Is it not only by a return to the Scriptures that the unity of the children of God can be manifested and the evangelisation of the world be accomplished?

In the beginning of the gospel there was no distinction between "home" and "foreign" work. Gradually, the spontaneous spread of the churches, irrespective of country and nationality, was modified by the change from primitive Apostolic churches to the organisation that developed from these, and "missions" began to be sent out representing the central authority that sent them. As organised Christian denominations multiplied, missions to other lands increased, each preaching Christ, but representing also its own particular scheme and development of Christianity, thus introducing among the heathen that confusion of conflicting sects from which Christendom suffers. The original way was not dependent upon material wealth, but on the power of the Holy Spirit, and was always connected with poverty. The methods that have developed are expensive, because the gifts of the Holy Spirit, who dwells in the newest believer and supplies the needs for testimony of the least company of disciples, are not recognised, a "Mission Station" being established to supply all needs. This has to be supported, and it becomes necessary to appeal for money at the "home base" or, where this is thought unworthy of faith, some reliance is placed for the awakening of interest in the work on the publication of moving incidents or distressing needs. In this way, too, the direction and support of the work "abroad" being largely in the hands of those "at home" or their representatives, it remains an alien institution in the land where it is carried on and the spread of the gospel is impeded to an incalculable degree.

Following Christ and denying self may well include readiness to sever the most cherished traditional ties that bind us to our different denominational organisations, and to find means of practicing genuine fellowship with all the Lord's people, exercising that forbearance with one another which our present weakness would necessitate. If we ourselves kept the teachings of Scripture, we might then put it into the hands of men of all nations and, by precept and example, show them

> that it is given for them as much as for us, in the sure belief that God would keep and guide them, and give them their place as independent churches and their inheritance among the saints.

This next paragraph is prophetic, I might say. It was written before brother Broadbent ever knew about Watchman Nee. In fact, I'm not even sure that brother Broadbent ever did know of either Bakht Singh or brother Nee.

> We do not know what gifts the Holy Spirit may awaken in places outside the scope of modern missionary activities and in circumstances manifestly beyond our power to control. The persecuted Russian churches have experiences beyond ours, and a zeal and devotion is quickened among them to which most professing Christians in easier circumstances are strangers; it may well be that in their midst, miracles of unity and testimony will be wrought such as we have failed to accomplish.

That's a testimony which has come true.

> Out of the heathen world, leaders may be raised up, so filled with the [Holy] Spirit that they will be able to leave behind both the divisions and the wealth of European and American Missions and will see conversions and the growth of churches of God among their own people, churches which may indeed have to learn from mistakes of their own, but will be free from ours [in the West]. With God nothing is impossible.

He might call, even out of Islam, submissive, devoted disciples of Christ whom He could use in His service among that people. All this does not leave out of account the value, beyond price, of the devotion and service that have so long flowed, and still [continues to] flow, through Missionary Societies and Institutions, to the world, but it envisages the multitudes that are unreached (and will remain unreached at the present rate of progress), pointing out the one way of revival, which is a return to the way of the word [of God].

God is manifested in Christ by the Holy Spirit as the Lover, [the] Seeker, [the] Saviour, and [the] Keeper of lost mankind. There is no revelation more affecting than this, that God is of such a nature that the misery of fallen man has constrained Him to lay aside His heavenly glory, to become Man, to bear all our sin and more than all our sorrow, and by death vanquish death and give to dying sinners eternal and divine life. Every one who by faith receives this life is under the same necessity as He from whom he derives it, so that on this account every Christian is naturally a missionary. He hears in his soul as an impelling command, the words, "Go ye into all the world and preach the gospel to every creature."

In the New Testament there is no distinction between clergy and laity, all the saints are priests. So also, there is no distinction between missionaries and non-missionaries—every believer is "sent," or has a "mission," to be a witness for Christ in the world. The formation of a separate missionary class grouped in missionary societies, supported by special mission funds, working through mission stations, though it has accomplished so much [for which we thank God], is dearly bought while it contents the vast bulk of Christians to be non-missionaries, and dims the vision of every saint as in every circumstance wholly the Lord's, and devoted first and last to His service. The aim of the gospel is the conversion of sinners into saints, and the gathering of these as churches. Since each member of a church is called to be a missionary, or witness for Christ, each church is a "missionary society," [or] a society of persons who are collectively engaged in the testimony of [Christ[2]].

The difference between a mission station and a church is that a mission station, with the missionary society of which it is a branch, is the centre to which the natives of the country in which it is, look for guidance and supplies. A church, on the other hand, in the New Testament sense of the word, is, from the moment of its beginning, when two or three are gathered in the Name of the Lord Jesus on the same foundation as the oldest established church, having the same Centre, [and] the same principles. Different, it is true, in gift and experience, it is yet partaker of the same grace, and draws its supplies from the same Source. Moreover, it is the most suitable instrument for the furtherance of the gospel among the people from which it has been called, and with whose thoughts, language, customs, and needs its members have perfect acquaintance. A mission station may be of great value, but should never be made the centre around which a church gathers: that centre is Jesus Christ. There is also a difference

2 Broadbent's words "the gospel."

between a church and an institution, such as a hospital or a school. These may be of the utmost value, commending the gospel, gaining the confidence of the people; but if a hospital or school, of foreign origin, comes to be regarded as the centre around which the church is gathered, and upon which it depends, such a church cannot develop according to the New Testament pattern. It remains a foreign religion dependent on supplies from abroad. It may even develop a system of salaried "native evangelists," destructive of dependence upon God, [and] hindering growth in learning to know Him.

Scripture does not lead us to expect that the gospel will prevail so as to bring about the conversion of the world; on the contrary, we are taught to look for increasing departure from God, bringing terrible judgments upon all the earth. The return of the Lord Jesus Christ in glory is the hope which is set before the Church. Awaiting that great event, we remember the Lord's last prayer for His disciples; "That they all may be one ... [and] that the world may believe that Thou hast sent Me."

These two things, the unity of the people of God and the making known of the Saviour in the world, are the desire of all who are in communion with the Lord. The history of the Church shows that revival comes through return to obedience to the word of God. This prayer of the Lord is certainly promised also; it will be accomplished [even] as He prayed. Doubtless the full accomplishment of it will be when He comes, but it may be that the last great revival [in world history] will be a foreshadowing even here on Earth, of that which is shortly to come to pass both in heaven and on Earth.

I found that very interesting in the light of what we said. Let us read it again: "Doubtless the full accomplishment of it," that is, that all may be one, and that the world may believe that Thou sent Me, "doubtless the full accomplishment of it will be when He comes, but it may be that the last great revival [in world history] will be a foreshadowing, even here on Earth, of that which is shortly to come to pass, both in heaven and on Earth."

When the disciples of the Lord repent and forsake ways that are ways of departure from His word, and gather as churches in immediate dependence upon Him, free from the bondage of human federations and organisations, and free to receive all who belong to Him, they will experience His sufficiency, as those did who went before them in this path [in the Pilgrim Church]; being delivered, on the one hand, from fellowship with unbelievers, and, on the other, from separation from fellow-saints.

Moreover, in taking the gospel to people of all nations and races, they will apprehend that the whole word of God is for others as well as for themselves; that all who believe are brought into the same relationship to Him, and that no difference of nationality can affect the standing of a church in the sight of God. The work of the Spirit in all will manifest the truth that Peter had learned when he said, "God, which knoweth the hearts, bare them witness, giving them the Holy Ghost, even as He did unto us; and put no difference between us and them, purifying their hearts by faith ... we believe that through the grace of the Lord Jesus Christ we shall be saved even as they."

As we review the long path already traversed by the Pilgrim Church, certain salient points appear. Rising above the mass of detail, so poignant at the time to those whose lives made it up, they rightly claim attention, for they turn the experience of the way that lies behind into guidance for the track that stretches before.

One is that the Pilgrim Church has possessed in the Scriptures a safe and sufficient guide for all the way from Pentecost to the present time, and has the assurance that it will suffice until that lamp shining in a dark place shall pale before the glory of the appearing of Him who is the Living Word (II Peter 1:19).

A second thought is that the Pilgrim Church is separate from the world; though in it is not of it, it never becomes an earthly institution. Though a witness to the world and a blessing in it, yet, since the world which crucified Christ does not change, and the disciple is content to be as his Master, the pilgrims still exhort one another with the words: "Let us go forth, therefore unto Him without the camp, bearing His reproach. For here have we no continuing city, but we seek one to come (Hebrews 13:13–14).

A third is that the Church is One. Insofar as we know ourselves to be members of the Pilgrim Church, we acknowledge as our fellow-pilgrims all who tread the Way of Life. Passing differences, however keen at the time, grow dim as we view the whole pilgrimage spread out before us. In deepest humility, as we think of the littleness of our own part, and with heartfelt delight in our fellows, we claim them as such. Their sufferings are ours, their testimony

> ours, because their Saviour, Leader, Lord and Hope is ours. By enlightening of the Holy Spirit we have learned, with them, to rejoice with the Father when He says, "This is My beloved Son, in whom I am well pleased" (Matthew 3:17). With them, too, we rejoice in the prospect of that day when the Son will present to Himself "a glorious church, not having spot or wrinkle or any such thing" (Ephesians 5:27)

Well, you may not entirely agree with that. That was published in 1931 for the first time. Broadbent was certainly a living example of what he wrote. He was an indefatigable labourer who gave his life, from the moment he was saved to the end, in tireless activity in the Lord, and has become the means of bringing so many churches into being in Siberia, which to this day have stood through the fiery test of the last 30 or 40 years. So, what he says does have weight, even though we may not agree with it all. All I can suggest is that you read *The Pilgrim Church* from beginning to end. I do not think you will find it a boring or a dull account at all. I think you will find it a very thrilling one. I know one or two have said they found it a bit too much, but I think it is a very exciting account.

The Heart of Everything is the Church

Christ's Pre-eminence

Well, now, just from that, there are one or two final observations that I would like to make.

One is that the heart of everything is the church. That sounds blasphemous, but it is not. It sounds blasphemous if we accept the modern conception of the church, but it is not when we understand the idea in Scripture. What the Holy Spirit has revealed to us as the church is something altogether different to the subconscious idea that we have of what we call the church.

Christ's pre-eminence in all things is linked with His being head of the body, which is the church. If you look at Colossians 1:17–18, it says quite clearly that "in all things ... He is the head of the body, the church: who is the beginning, the firstborn from the dead; that in all things He might have the pre-eminence.

It is interesting that the Holy Spirit has linked these things: head of the body, the beginning, the firstborn from the dead, that in all things He might have the pre-eminence. The pre-eminent place of Christ, the supreme place of the Lord Jesus, is linked with the church, with His being head of the body. That is the most important point. For instance, we can maybe take another step in that the headship of Christ, the lordship of Christ is really a church matter. If you and I accept the Lord Jesus as Lord, we immediately become related to other Christians. You cannot really accept the lordship or headship of Christ without becoming vitally related to brothers and sisters. The whole concept in Scripture of His being head and we being the body means that each member has got to be rightly related to the other members in order to be in direct link and contact with the head.

The Body of Christ

My body is made up of a multitude of members. Each member is directly linked by my nervous system with my brain, with my head. But in fact, if you were to dissect my body, you would discover that all the many parts have got to be related to all the other parts in order to be directly linked with the head. Now this is exactly what the Holy Spirit has tried to get over to people when He has described Christ and the church as the head and the body.

To really accept the Lord Jesus as Lord and head means that we have to come into relationship to our brothers and sisters; not in a theoretical way, but in a real, genuine, practical and down to earth way. I cannot overemphasise that, for the Scripture reveals to us quite clearly that the church is Christ.

Therefore, when we say that the heart of everything is the church, we are in fact saying that Christ is the centre and the heart of everything. He is the head over all things, the Lord of all. But if you look through Scripture, you will begin to discover that all the whole world being brought under the headship of Christ, all the other things being reconciled to God, is linked first with the Lord Jesus producing a people: the church.

If you look at 1 Corinthians 12:12, you get this little phrase, "so also is Christ" that we often mention. If you look at Romans 12:5, you will discover again the same little phrase, "so also is Christ." We, being many members, are yet one body, so also is Christ. The many members comprise Christ. He is Himself the head, but His body is just as much part of Him.

That is a tremendous point. When we begin to see what the church really is, not in our traditional conception, but in God's conception. What does He mean by this word *church*? He means that just as you have a head and just as you have a body, so Christ is the head and we are the body. We are essentially part of one life, of one great entity, of one great unity, if you like, by redemption, by new birth, by the Holy Spirit. We have been made partakers of Christ, members of Christ. We have become His very flesh and bone.

Sometimes when you start to talk along this line, people begin to think that you are getting unbalanced. But it is amazing how, in fact, we have a remarkable capacity for overlooking a large number of scriptures which deal with this whole point.

The True Nature of the Church

Christ as the Vine, We as the Branches

So, I want to underline it. For instance, in John 15, the Lord Jesus Himself gave us the basis for all Paul's doctrine of the church. You cannot, just as it were, throw it out as a Pauline conception. The Lord Jesus said, "I am the vine, ye are the branches." But what is a vine?

A vine is almost wholly made up of branches. At least, if you have ever been in the East and seen the little vine straggling, it is nearly all branches; just a little knob, and out of it come the branches. Jesus said, "I am the vine, ye are the branches." But when He said, "I am the vine," He meant, "I am the totality of the vine. I am the root, I am the little trunk, I am the branches, I am the leaves, I am the blossom, I am the fruit, I *am* the vine. But ye are the branches." When you begin to understand the Lord's own words, you have come for the first time into a glimmer of what the mystery is, which Paul called the mystery hid from all ages, this remarkable mystery that somehow or other we are in Christ and Christ is in us. But one step further, it is not that we are just in Christ and Christ is in us, but we have become part of Christ.

Just as He said, "I am the vine, ye are the branches." Try and work it out! Our little finite minds say, "Now, just wait. Either He must be it, or we are it. We cannot both be it!" But that is just the point. That is where the Lord Jesus was trying to lead His disciples to the first basic understanding they ever had of what this is that you call the church. You see, He was saying, "I am the church and you are the church. I am the totality of the church. Everything is, in fact, derived from Me. Its character, its source, its energy, its constitution, its very meaning. It is all Me. Yet in some marvellous, wonderful way, you are the church."

The Lord Jesus again took this up in other ways when He said, "I am the light of the world," and "Ye are the light of the world." Not two kinds of light. He is the light and we are the light. He is the vine; we are the branches. We are in the vine.

He is the church. Yet we are the church. He is the head; we are the body. In all these different illustrations, you are coming back to the one great basic fact that what we describe in human language as the church is the most remarkable fact in the whole universe. For it is bound up with the very Son of God Himself.

By redemption, you and I have been made partakers of Him. Not that we might live our own little individualistic lives, and receive a little bit of Christ into our old man, but that by our old man having been crucified with Christ, we might now come into a new life altogether. We might, by receiving Him, become part of Him, and become, as it were, the very body of God. If you like, the church is the container of God, in the same way that my body is the container of my personality. It is the means, the vessel, by which I express myself, by which you see me.

Why, if I was present with you and speaking to you without my body, it would be a very remarkable time altogether. Some of you would probably have a very difficult time just listening to a voice coming out of the air. You see, the whole point is that God has so ordered, constituted us that we have what we call a body which expresses our inner person, our inner man. Our personality is expressed through our body. Now, when the Holy Spirit took this term up, he was only taking up finite human terms.

We must never, ever forget this fact: that Scripture, although it is wonderful, and it is the word of God which abideth forever, is nevertheless human language. It is as if the Holy Spirit has wrestled with human language, to try and put into terms and words which we can understand what God is and what He has done and what we have become through Calvary and the resurrection and Pentecost.

Therefore, you see, we take the term "body." Some of us imagine somehow the church is a kind of body. But all Paul was doing when he described the church as the body was to say that this body is a system. It is a unity. It is a vessel, a container, a means of expression.

Now, the church is just like that, you see. It is a unity. It is a container; it is a vessel. It is something through which God can express Himself. He lives in it. Just like you live in your body, so God wants to live in the church. It is His mode of expression, if you like. I don't know how else you can approach it.

So, when you begin to understand that, you begin to come to an understanding of what the church really means. Never divorce the church from Christ. When you do that, it is the beginning of all the trouble. Always, whenever you think of the church, think of it as Christ.

Alright, go right back to the seed plot of all this. When Christ said again about the vine, "abide in Me and I in you," that is the church. You and I leave the ground of our own individualism and get into Christ. Christ becomes the foundation and the basis of our living.

Then Christ is in us and He becomes the new life and nature and character of our being. Do you understand? Now, if all of us get into Christ, we are all found in the same place, and if Christ gets into all of us, then a strange thing has happened. One person is in us all and all of us are in one person. Do you understand? That is the church!

That is the whole concept of the ecclesia or the "called-out ones." They have been called out into Christ, and Christ is now in them. When that is understood, you have begun to understand this word, *church*.

Therefore, you see, to be Christ-centred is to be church-centred. That is all. You cannot be centred in Christ and not centred in the church. You cannot have Christ as head and not be properly and genuinely related to your brothers and sisters and you must not just think that that means a little group here. Practically, it means those who are prepared to be built together wherever we are, that we have to be built together. But you know, it means that if you and I are out of gear with any Christian anywhere in the world, the life is hindered.

Avoiding the Danger of Exclusivism

The Lesson from Jonah

Some of us have a weird idea that as long as we are all right with everyone in the little company we are with, we can say "Oh, that is wonderful. The Lord is with us. He will bless us, He will keep us, He will use us," and all the rest of it. But you know, I can think the most terrible things about brother so-and-so or sister so-and-so who is 500 miles away, or 100 miles away, or 50 miles away, or even 3 miles away, or even in the same locality, but not coming to the same company. I can say anything, do anything, feel anything, but somehow "that is alright, the Lord will bless you." But you see, that is just where you are wrong. The church consists of every true born-again believer alive, as well as those in the glory.

Therefore, you see, practically, you and I have to be related and built together with those who are prepared to come onto the same ground of Christ—to be together. But beyond that, it means that you and I cannot afford to be out of gear with anyone. Any harsh attitude, any exclusive attitude, any superior attitude, any divisive attitude is immediately a check on the Holy Spirit.

You see, the whole root of this thing comes down to what we see in the book of Jonah: exclusivism. Exclusivism. It is the great danger of seeing something when so many people don't understand what the church is and as we have read in this wonderful account of those in every generation who have seen what the church is and have been obedient to the Lord. When you begin to see it, the greatest danger is exclusivism. You cannot help feeling, "Why doesn't everyone else see it?

Why? Why? Why? Why?" Gradually a superior spirit begins to develop. You look down your nose at the others and–well, you would lovingly serve those in the same company, sometimes, but you certainly would not lovingly serve all the saints. Do you understand what I mean? The rest of them, they are outsiders. They are outsiders.

Being Related to All Believers

So, you get this amazing mentality that you can believe in what we call the church and yet speak of some of the Lord's people as outsiders and some of them as insiders and it is a denial of the whole thing.

So, you see, here you are up against the great problem. To be Christ-centred is to be church-centred. But do we really understand what this term *church* means, that we talk about so often? We think we understand in our minds, but in experience and attitude we deny the very thing we believe.

Thus it was with Jonah, that dear man who represented the Lord and was the ambassador of the Lord and was perfectly happy to represent the Lord and speak to the Lord whatever the cost amongst His own people in Israel. As soon as he found the Lord had interests further afield, he closed down on the spot.

It wasn't that he was being malicious. It wasn't even that he thought he was being unkind. He just felt the Lord was wrong. That is all.

So began the great contention of the Lord with Jonah and Jonah with the Lord. Jonah felt the Lord was wrong and the Lord felt Jonah was wrong. Of course, we know who was right. But it is an amazing thing that many of us are just like that. We will not, of course, admit it. We would never say the Lord is wrong. But in our hearts, we find it very, very, very hard to accept what the Lord does when it is contrary to what we have said or what we feel.

Somehow or other, we have got little safety mechanisms that give us a way of escape when we see it happening and we say, "Oh, well, it cannot be. There must be some other explanation for it. It cannot be the Lord," and so on.

The Church at the Centre of God's Purpose

The Church as Heart of Creation

So, it is very important for us to understand that the heart of everything is the church. Christ in His body is the very heart of the creation. You may or may not accept this, but we believe that this world was brought into being, this whole universe was brought into being for what we call the church. In other words, if there had been no fall, we probably would not have had the term *church*. We would have just called it, perhaps, man. That is all. We call it church because there is a fallen man and then there is a new man. There is an old man and there is a new man. The new man is what God calls the church. But at the very beginning, when there was no old man, but only a new man, the whole concept of God was, "Now this man is on probation, but there is a tree of life and if he takes the tree of life, he comes into Me and I come into him." Then, you are immediately introduced to marriage. This is going to be the relationship; it is symbolised in marriage between the Son of God, the second person of the Trinity, and man. They are going to be united together so that man becomes the focal point of the natural creation's unity with

God, the means by which God controls and governs the natural creation, and the means by which the natural creation reaches God. Man was the great link.

One often speculates what would have happened if there had been no fall, if Adam and Eve had taken the tree of life. Well, they would have been without sin. They would have received the Holy Spirit and would have become a new creation. You see, when they were first created, they were created sinless but not perfect. Do you understand? Sinless, but not perfect. Sinless, but not complete.

They had to find out for themselves that they needed God. There was an emptiness, and it begins to come out when Adam, by himself, is shown all the natural creation. You see? "I've got a vacuum inside. I cannot understand. I've got a vacuum inside." He did not look for the tree and in the end, Eve came out and filled the vacuum. But, you know, after a while, if there had been no fall, Adam and Eve would have found a vacuum, and then they would have been forced back to the tree of life. Now, some of the old Puritan commentators have discovered, within Eve's readiness to take the tree of the knowledge of good and evil, an awakening sense, already, of a vacuum.

Adam was not enough. She, with the woman's greater perceptiveness and intuition, had already begun to sense that there was something much more to life than just Adam, wonderful as Adam was.

You know as well as I do that, if she had been absolutely satisfied with Adam, any serpent speaking to her would not have done much. She would have gone back to Adam, I am quite sure, and talked it over with him. But the point was that she felt a vacuum and, no doubt, so did Adam, because immediately when she spoke to him about this tree of the knowledge of good and evil (and he was not a fool) he accepted it. She knew what she was doing when she took that tree. "Ye shall be as God." Eve knew, she somehow had become aware that there was something of a little vacuum. See?

Now, just supposing she had not done that and had been forced back to the tree of life. Well, the whole course of history would have been different. We would have begun right back there in what we now call the church, only without sin! There would not have been any of this terrible conflict over our old natures. So, you see, the whole heart of the creation has to do with that. Christ in His body, is not only in the heart of creation, it is the very heart of history.

The Church as Heart of History

When you take books like I and II Chronicles, you know, it goes right back to Adam and goes right on to Christ and spans the whole of history. Why do we have two big books in the Bible which tell us all that the other books have told us anyway? What a waste of time and words! Why does the Holy Spirit sit down and write history all over again? Because He wanted us to understand that the temple, as it is called continually in Chronicles, is the heart, symbolically, of history, of Old Testament history, going right back to Adam and right on to Christ. The heart of it is this dwelling place of God. Well, that is only a symbol, of course, of the church: the body of Christ. It just was a picture of that. So, you see, the whole of history has, as its heart, Christ and His body.

Daniel is the one, of course, who takes this up supremely. He shows us all the great empires of Gentile world history and gradually he traces them right the way down. We discover that the heart of it all is His saints possessing the kingdom forever and ever. He paints for us a picture so dark, so black, with the balance so overwhelmingly on the side of evil and of Satan. Yet, in the end, it is the church which comes out on top.

Christ and His body are the heart of history. It has been the heart of history, of course, in the last centuries since Pentecost. We are still in the vision of Daniel, and every time you note that evil systems have started to tamper with the church—well, in the end, though they may seem to have succeeded, it is the Lord Jesus who triumphs. So, it will be in the very finish. So, Christ and His body are the heart of history. Human history is literally bounded by this church.

As soon as the last one is brought out and saved, human history as we know it will be ended and the Lord will come. He is only holding back, as it says in Scripture, because He is not willing that any should perish, but that all should come to repentance. The Lord Jesus will hold back for longer if there is one person that can be brought out of darkness into light.

The Church as Heart of Redemption

Then again, Christ and His body are the heart of redemption. If you look in Ephesians 5, you will discover that it speaks of Christ loving the church and giving Himself for the church, that He might present it to Himself, a church without spot or wrinkle or blemish or any such thing. So, redemption, the very heart of redemption, is the question of what we call the body of the Lord Jesus.

So you see, we can just go on. Service: take this question of service. Service, sacrificial service—the heart of it all is the church. If you read this great commission of the Lord Jesus, "Go ye into all the world and preach the gospel to every nation, to all nations, to every creature."

If you read on, the book of Acts, is the exemplification of that; the illustration of the initial fulfilling of that commission and where does it all centre? In the church.

Men go out from the church. Take Antioch: Paul and Barnabas go out from the church. When they go out, what happens? They proclaim Christ and then they gather all those who believe into what they call the church, and everywhere they go, they just simply leave the church behind them in those different places. Those churches become themselves the centres of evangelistic activity and testimony wherever they are, so that Paul could write a letter to the church at Thessalonica and say, "From you, the word of life has sounded forth into the whole of Achaia."

You see, the whole concept is that first, the preaching by which men are saved; they are being built together; and then they become themselves a centre by which others are brought in and saved. As Paul says, they will come amongst you and fall down and will worship, saying, "God is here."

So, you can go on and go on. It is true to say that Christ in His body is the heart of a new heaven and a new earth. When you come to the end of the Bible, you have got a new city, a new Jerusalem, and it is the heart of a new heaven and a new earth. It is in between the two and it rules and governs everything. It is the heart of it all.

What a tremendous thing the church is.

It is Christ—all that He set His heart upon.

The Need for Recovery of the Church

So you see, out of that comes another point: that is, that the recovery of the true nature, the organic constitution and the function of the church is of the greatest necessity. It is of the greatest necessity that the church of the Lord Jesus, the body of the Lord Jesus, its organic constitution and nature, should be recovered amongst God's own.

That is the point. It has been sadly compromised and lost. How few of us understand this situation that is mentioned not once, but hundreds of times in Scripture, and even so few of us understand it. We have been saved into it, and still we do not understand it. Isn't it amazing?

The heart of it all! God's great method, if I may say so, is the church. His method is the church. Get that clear into your hearts and then take the multitudes of Christians in the world in this 20th century, how many of them could tell you what the church is? We have been saved into it, and we do not know what we are saved into!

The greatest necessity is the recovery of the church.

Now, don't get it wrong. We are not saying this in a kind of introspective way. Someone suggested to me that in saying this, "Aren't we being introspective? You see, the commission of the church is to go out, not to just try and put itself into order all the time." But I want to question that. You see, our great point is that if the house itself is all upside down, there is no point in going out. The thing is to tackle the heart of the problem, and the rest will take shape.

Now, let me explain it like this. Supposing we could, by the Holy Spirit, reproduce something, not as an imitation, but originally and organically like that at Pentecost. Well, we would exceed all the missionary activity of the last 10 years within a few weeks.

When you take the book of Acts, which covers just a few years, you have the whole of an empire traversed from end to end and in the sub-apostolic era, you have missionaries going right out to India. Indeed, tradition tells us that it was one of the apostles himself who died the martyr's death in India. Taking the gospel right down to the farthest tip of India and right out farther afield you had them going, all within literally half a century.

Then you think of our heavy work, so painful and so slow—we are not being critical, but we are just stating a fact. The money that goes into it, the manpower that is in it, the interest that is in it. Why, it just doesn't bear any comparison with the New Testament. If the New Testament had all the wealth, and the money, and the interest, and the backing, and the manpower that we have in the 20th century, I don't know what would have happened. But you see, with all this, we are still not really producing the simple, eternal, heavenly results of the first 20 years of church history.

Now that is what I just simply mean when we say that the greatest necessity is the recovery of the nature of the church. I don't think it is introspective at all. I believe it is being absolutely sound. If your car is beginning to crack up and fall to pieces, the right thing to do is to get the thing put right. Not just to go on and on and on and on until finally the thing just drops into a heap in the middle of some road somewhere. You have to put it right. Isn't that so? I mean, supposing we looked at the state of our building, we just said it is no good, it is not a good time to put it right. It's got dry rot, got everything else wrong with it, it's got no electricity, nothing else. You go through the floor and everything else. But let's carry on. Come on. We've got to get people in. We've got to. So we pack them in, and suddenly the whole thing falls and we are all killed. There is no point in it!

The thing you do is tackle the basic things first and the rest takes shape. So it is with this. It is of tremendous importance that the church should be recovered and I think that is what we must underline in this. It is sane and balanced to review and to examine what we are really in as Christians and whether, in fact, what we are saved into is functioning.

Then you see how important all that is. Recovery of the church, the nature, organic constitution, and function of the church is necessary for God's purpose. It is really necessary for God's purpose, it is necessary for the effective evangelism, and it is necessary for the building up of God's own: three essential points which necessitate the recovery of the church.

I think we ought to note the great amount of Scripture that is taken up with this theme of recovery. When you take the prophets' ministry, you have to recognise, because scholars of varying shades of thought all agree on this, that the main emphasis of their ministry is recovery. Something has been lost. Before we can do anything else, we have to go back to it. It is no good Israel trying to proselytise the nations. The Lord Jesus Himself said, you are putting the cart before the horse. You make them worse than yourselves.

The thing is, put the nation right at the heart, then go out; this is the burden of the prophets. So they began with judgment, terrible judgment, and woes. Then they went on to the promise of restoration and blessing and they nearly always finally ended with all the nations flowing into Zion. Most of the prophets' ministry is based on that simple division.

First, judgment. Then, the promise of restoration if there's repentance and finally, all the nations flowing into Zion and into Jerusalem, and the Lord, as it were, saving the nations. You have got that in all the prophets. So, I do trust that you see something of the necessity of the church being recovered. So, I come back to what I am, in these few final observations, seeking to underline, that the pouring out of the Holy Spirit is the only answer to such a necessity. If the church, in its organic constitution, is to be recovered, then it needs a pouring out of the Holy Spirit.

Early Rain and Latter Rain

It is very interesting that Scripture speaks of the early rain and the latter rain. James, in speaking of the return of the Lord Jesus, says that the farmer, the husbandman, has patience "for the early and the latter rain." Then he says, "You also establish your hearts. The coming of the Lord draweth near." Isn't that interesting that he should speak of early and latter rain in connection with the Lord's return? The coming of the Lord drawing near—the fruits.

Is there not perhaps something there for you and I to follow up? Is there not a hearkening back to the prophecies of Joel? We spoke of the dual nature of Joel's ministry. We have read the scene in that tremendous vision of the valley of the dry bones that Ezekiel had. Oh, it was impossible. Supposing I had gone to Ezekiel and said, "Ezekiel," as he stood up there viewing all those dead, dry bones, "Well, Ezekiel, you know, the Lord's got to have this, all these bones as a people."

He would say, "It's impossible."

Well, I should say to him, "If the Lord Jesus is to return, something has got to happen to these dry bones."

The key was the Holy Spirit; the word of God and the Holy Spirit, and it all happened. It was a miracle. It was supernatural, but it happened.

Prayer is the Key to Revival

So, I believe Pentecost is the character of the New Testament age, as we have said. It may well be that it is, obviously not in the same initial character of Pentecost, but there may well be a corresponding counterpart that will end or close this age.

So, I say that there is a very great need for the most urgent and relentless prayer, for such an outpouring of the hope that is based on Scripture. If you folk did nothing else but went back and started to search the Scriptures on this point, I think your prayer life would be transformed. You would have the solid rock, the impregnable rock of God's word under your feet in prayer.

Again and again, the key to all this is prayer. May I just say that we ought to be very careful of despising the prayer in so many different circles of God's children for revival. We may feel at times it is misguided, and in some quarters that is true. People want to fill their churches, that is all. It is true that in some quarters it is so, but not so in the majority. There is a great concern in many of God's children's hearts. They, perhaps, do not understand what we mean by the church. They do not understand much about God's great eternal purpose. But they've got eyes to see this far: that something is empty, something is wrong. So they are doing the right thing and saying, "Lord, revive Thy work."

It has always been that when people have called upon the Lord to do this, He has answered them, not according to their asking, but according to His own word. When Evan Roberts started to pray for revival, he had no idea what it entailed. It smashed him up as well as Wales. It is that people who pray, do not really know what they are praying. It may be that they have, in their mentality, their own little gospel hall or mission or something else being filled and blessed and so on. But when it comes, it is entirely different. Sometimes it sweeps the whole thing away. When John and Charles Wesley and Whitefield prayed for an outpouring of the Holy Spirit, if you said to them, "You know it is going to sweep you out of the church of England," they would say, "Then we won't have a revival!" But the point was, they went on praying because they knew there was a concern. It came and swept them out. That is always what happens.

Thus it has been in every move of God's Holy Spirit. You begin by asking the Lord for something. You've got your own little concern, conceptions of what it means, how the Lord's going to answer and what it will mean. But when it happens, it is entirely different.

Don't despise prayer for revival. Encourage it everywhere. Encourage it. Let people know that you are with them in their prayer for this outpouring of God's Holy Spirit. Because when it comes, it will not come to just a few, it will come to all. It will be upon all, as in every single outpouring of the Holy Spirit. I think that we should remember that. It is a very, very great thing.

If God can take hold of a man like Saul on his way to Damascus, intent on killing people left, right and centre, and in one single hour change him from the great persecutor of the church into the great apostle of the church, I do not believe that the 20th century presents any great difficulties to God.

He can do exactly the same. I do believe that God could take hold of a man like Nikita Khrushchev and save him in an hour if He wanted to do so. But the key to it all is the faithful devotion and prayer of God's people—you and I.

The dear C.T. Studd said, "Why ask God for an egg if you can ask Him for an elephant?" Most of us are asking God for eggs. "Oh, give us little things," because somehow or other we cannot believe that God could do a big thing. But I do believe that the prayer of faith is to take hold of the Lord, inwardly knowing that He can do very much bigger things than we ask.

Don't we confine the Lord to what we think might be possible? What is in our own experience? I think so. I have never heard anyone here pray that Khrushchev might be converted. I have not prayed for him myself. But is it because we do not believe it is possible? Why, church history is full of such things: men who are violently against the Lord suddenly being apprehended by God and turned right round to the opposite. It is hard to believe, isn't it? But with God, nothing is impossible. If women can turn to flight armies of aliens, through faith, well, why can't something happen when there are people who really trust in the Lord?

So, I hope that you will take these final observations I have made. Insofar as we have left all that divides and are on the ground simply of Christ, and are seeking to be obedient to the Lord Jesus Christ and His word and the Holy Spirit, to give the Holy Spirit His sovereign place amongst us, we are in the apostolic succession of the pilgrim church. Poor and weak we may be, but we are in the apostolic succession of the pilgrim church, and therefore also in a mighty conflict.

You know, every big thing begins with a little thing. Remember that.

A breakthrough always begins with a little trickle. Read church history. Read this *Pilgrim Church*, if you like. It always begins with a little trickle and the devil's whole point is blocked by a little trickle. If you do not stop that little trickle, you have wrecked everything.

You all know the wonderful Dutch story of the little lad who was out one day running along the dikes, and he found a small little hole with a little trickle coming through, and he knew what that meant. If that hole was left for another two hours in the great dike that held out the sea, it would gradually become a great hole. The whole thing would collapse and hundreds of miles of fenland would be swamped by sea water. So the little lad put his arm into the hole and stemmed it off.

Do you understand what I mean? A little trickle is the beginning. The devil's got a big dam that he is going to dike, if you like, and one little trickle cannot be left by him for long. It wears it down and gradually the whole thing collapses and out flows a huge river of life.

No, we ought to recognize that Satan's out to deviate us and he will deviate us in any way that is possible as long as he can get us off the path. If he cannot do it from without, he will do it from within.

If he cannot do it from division within, then he will do it by continual wearing down of our attitude to the Lord and His people until in the end, unbeknownst to ourselves, we become a little exclusive in-turned group who are standing for the truth concerning the church. Europe's scattered with them, little groups standing for the truth concerning the church and the Lord never does a thing in or with them. That is why it is tragic.

They never pray for anyone to be saved. They never pray for the Lord's other people; they are all wrong. Yet they have seen something, so they feel.

Renewing Our First Love

No, our greatest need is a renewal in first love. That is our greatest need. It will result in three things: a passion for the unsaved and a new love for all God's children; and it will result in a preparedness for and a committal to being built together. You will never get it without love. Never. That is the problem with so many of us. We cannot even pray for unsaved people because we have got no real love for them and we know it.

We also seem to be afraid to pray for renewal of love. That is what we need, a renewal of love that will just break down the whole thing and at least put us into a position to pray for the Lord to do something.

Oh, do listen to what I have to say. We need a minute re-examination of our whole history, of all that we believe; not in an introspective way, but a re-examination and assessment of everything. There are some things we had in the beginning which are counteracted now by feelings and ideas that, when we really get down to it, we should not have.

It needs re-examination and assessment before the Lord, with the Holy Spirit in charge. It needs also, thirdly, a great prayer ministry that will take hold of the Lord in these days and really, really pray into being the promises that God has made in His word.

I do not know whether you really believe what I say, but there you are. If there had not been a Daniel to pray into being the return to the land, there would have been no real return, as far as I can make out. If there had not been others who prayed and prayed other things into being, it would never have happened. Somewhere or other, there is always God's link on earth with anything He does from heaven.

So it is with us. But you cannot do it without love. Try. You cannot do it. If you try, it will only show up the emptiness that is in us. No, we have to be forced to a new appeal to the Lord to renew our first love and in that way, I believe, we will discover that the Lord Himself is able to do a much deeper and fuller thing in us all.

8. The Manifestation of the Spirit

1 Corinthians 12:4–11 NASB
Now there are varieties of gifts, but the same Spirit. And there are varieties of ministries, and the same Lord. And there are varieties of effects, but the same God who works all things in all persons. But to each one is given the manifestation of the Spirit for the common good. For to one is given the word of wisdom through the Spirit, and to another the word of knowledge according to the same Spirit; to another faith by the same Spirit, and to another gifts of healing by the one Spirit, and to another the effecting of miracles, and to another prophecy, and to another the distinguishing of spirits, to another various kinds of tongues, and to another the interpretation of tongues. But one and the same Spirit works all these things, distributing to each one individually just as He wills.

Romans 8:26–27
And in like manner the Spirit also helpeth our infirmity: for we know not how to pray as

we ought; but the Spirit himself maketh intercession for us with groanings which cannot be uttered; and he that searcheth the hearts knoweth what is the mind of the Spirit, because He maketh intercession for the saints according to the will of God.

All true and genuine corporate prayer is a manifestation of the Presence of the Holy Spirit. The Greek word translated by the English word *manifestation* literally means "to make visible, or observable; to make known, or to make clear." Essentially, it has the idea of uncovering, of laying bare, or of revealing a matter. When we understand this, we begin to comprehend the real meaning of the manifestation of the Spirit. The Holy Spirit is uncovering the mind and the will of the Head—revealing His burden and concern. The aim of the Spirit is to enable us, through the spiritual weapons which He supplies to us, to realise a successful outcome or to take executive action when necessary. Sometimes in prayer we only dimly understand what the mind of the Lord is on any given matter, because His mind is not clear to us. The manifestation of the Spirit however gives crystal clarity to our time of corporate prayer. Sometimes we only need to know what we are up against; we may feel all kinds of currents in the atmosphere. It may be a heaviness, or an onslaught of the powers of darkness, or it may be something else; but we are not aware as to what those currents might be. Other times we are not clear as to what the goal and aim of the Lord is in particular situations.

It is the grace of God when there is a manifestation of the

Spirit through which we come to a revelation of the mind of the Lord. If the Lord Jesus has been made Head over all things to the church, then it seems only spiritually logical to expect that He will make known practically how we are to pray and proceed. The uncovering and laying bare of the heart of God is the strategic significance of the manifestation of the Spirit.

We are told that this manifestation of the Spirit is for the "common good" (NASB), "to profit withal" (AV and ASV). The Spirit of God manifests Himself to the advantage of the whole body. It is interesting to note that "to each one is given the manifestation of the Spirit." It is in fact the body of Christ in action or the members of His body functioning as they should. Furthermore, if there is to be an outcome to our prayer through the Holy Spirit, we need to be harmonised, to be together, or to be "agreed." Thus a time of corporate prayer becomes a thermometer of the health of a congregation or a fellowship. If we do not know how to move together, we are merely a collection of individuals saved by His grace but strangers to the functioning of His body.

We are urged by the apostle Paul: "With all prayer and supplication praying at all seasons in the Spirit." As we have already explained in chapter four such "praying in the Spirit" can only be experienced when we are under the sovereign leading and enabling power of the Holy Spirit (see Ephesians 6:18). It is a spiritual dimension into which we enter; it is His burden that is conceived in us; He is the One who prompts us, leads us, and enables us to pray. That means we are under and in the anointing of the Spirit. He is also the One who harmonises us and empowers us not only to understand what the will of God is but to see His will fulfilled in practice on this fallen earth. Corporate prayer is thus in the realm and dimension of the Spirit of God. If that is true, then there must be times when the Holy Spirit manifests Himself in specific ways.

The Gifts of the Spirit

The gifts of the Spirit are the equipment, the tools, and the weapons with which we can accomplish the work. Whilst these gifts apply to much more than corporate prayer, they are strategic and vital to such prayer if the Lord is to direct us accurately and efficiently. No one would think of fixing a car engine with a paint brush or of trying to paint a house with a wrench. One needs the right tools! It would be a shock if one had to have an appendix operation, and the surgeon came with a tree saw and a mallet. If a patient were to ask him, "Why have you come with a tree saw and a mallet?" It would be no small shock to hear him say, "The mallet is to knock you out, and the tree saw is to cut you open!" One would feel that he was not in possession of the right equipment! When we have the right equipment, or the correct weapons for the time of prayer, the work that the Lord wants us to do can be done properly and efficiently.

The Holy Spirit manifests Himself in many ways. In corporate prayer He uses a number of the gifts which He manifests amongst us. By the Holy Spirit Paul, in fact, writes of nine gifts: The *word of wisdom,* the *word of knowledge, faith,* the *gifts of healing,* the *effecting of miracles, prophecy,* the *distinguishing of spirits, various kinds of tongues,* and the *interpretation of tongues* (see 1 Corinthians 12:8–10 NASB). All of these are to the advantage of the whole body—to its building up, its functioning, and its spiritual health. Some of those gifts are particularly useful in corporate prayer. Let us consider some of them.

The Word of Knowledge

For example, in corporate prayer a word of knowledge can be a key to unlocking so much. It is the explanation of the facts in any situation, problem, circumstance, or satanic onslaught. To know those facts is at least fifty percent of the way towards victory. Many times we are completely nonplussed by situations which confront a fellowship or an assembly, or which confront the work of the Lord, and we cannot make any headway at all. The reason is that we are ignorant of the facts. To know the facts in any given situation may immensely help us, but it is not the full answer.

The Word of Wisdom

A word of wisdom can change the whole atmosphere of a time of corporate prayer. The manifestation of the Spirit in a word of wisdom gives us the understanding of how to *handle* the facts. This means that we are seventy-five percent of the way towards victory. Simply because we have knowledge of the facts of any situation or problem does not mean that we know how to proceed in prayer. To know how to handle those facts means that we can proceed with great confidence in the Lord and witness the fulfilment of our prayer.

In the early part of the Yom Kippur War in Israel in 1973, a number of local believers had met together in Jerusalem for intercession. The war was in a "touch and go" state. The matter that was so much on the hearts of Israel's Defence Minister, Moshe Dayan, and the Chief of Staff, David Elazar, was the possibility that the Hashemite Kingdom of Jordan would join Syria and Egypt in attacking Israel. Of all our neighbours, Jordan has the longest border with Israel.

We were praying with great passion and purpose when suddenly Colonel Orde Dobbie broke in to our prayer with the words: "Would you all please judge this? Three times I have seen the same picture of large clouds coming down and blotting out the mountains of Moab. (The Mountains of Moab are in modern day Jordan.) I do not understand it, but I wonder does it have some meaning for our prayer time?" Orde Dobbie was not an emotional man and was from a military family, which for many generations had served in the British army. We all began to pray that the Lord would show us whether this was from the Lord and what it signified. Suddenly one of those present said, "Should we not pray that Jordan will be so confused by the Lord that they will not enter this war?" If Jordan had come into the war, in all likelihood, it would have tilted the war in favour of the Arabs. We all felt that we should pray in that manner, and we did with great fervour. The Hashemite Kingdom of Jordan, in fact, never came into the Yom Kippur War and was roundly criticized for not doing so by Syria, Egypt, and other Arab states.

At least a month later I was staying with my mother in the family home in Richmond, England, when I suddenly heard my mother calling my name and saying, "Lance, come down quickly. King Hussein is being interviewed on the television." I came down in time to hear the interviewer saying, "But, your majesty, you must know that all the Arab states around you are criticizing you for not coming into that war." King Hussein replied, "We had made the decision to enter the war, but suddenly, we became greatly confused by the fact that we did not have sufficient air cover, and thus we decided we could not enter it."

This is a good illustration of the Holy Spirit manifesting a word of knowledge and then a word of wisdom, and thus leading us all in prayer, with perfect result.

The Gift of Faith

When the Holy Spirit manifests Himself in a gift of faith, and it is expressed, it can make all the difference between defeat and failure or victory. Many times in corporate prayer the expression of God given faith spells a breakthrough, and the realisation of victory. There are many occasions when one has witnessed this. After much prayer, sometimes prolonged prayer, suddenly one child of God expresses with their lips their faith that the Lord has heard and answered. Almost immediately, there is a witness in others that it is true; and the prayer time changes from earnest appeal and petition, or spiritual warfare, to praise and worship.

In one prayer time in Jerusalem, when we were in prayer concerning a very prickly and complex situation, which seemed to be as unyielding as iron, someone expressed their faith that we had been heard and that the Lord would act. We then began to praise and thank the Lord. One of the brothers took down a large and ancient shofar which was hanging on the wall, and gave it to another brother who could blow it properly. When he blew the shofar, the sound resonated in the spirits of all who were present and lifted us onto another level. We saw in the weeks that followed the practical answer to that prayer; and we worshipped the Lord.

The Discernment of Spirits

In many situations which are being raised in corporate prayer, there are some problems that are very complex. On occasions when no solution can be found for a problem, and it is unusually complex, more often than not it is a sign that there is demonic influence involved. Sometimes it is more than an influence; it is a bondage which appears to be unbreakable; a blockage which is immovable. It is here that the manifestation of the Spirit in the gift of discerning or distinguishing spirits is vital. Once there is a demonic hold on the problem, it cannot be broken or moved until we recognise and know which kind of spirit is involved. The word of God is absolutely clear on this: "That through death He might bring to nought him that hath the power of death, that is, the devil; and might deliver all them ..." (Hebrews 2:14b–15a). The finished work of the Messiah spells total victory over all the works of the Devil involved in situations, problems, or in people. Once we know what we are facing in the problems, we can stand firmly on the finished work of the Messiah and see the demonic grip and hold on them broken.

Prophecy

Many times international, national, or even local situations appear dark and confusing, and we cannot make head or tail of them. When the Holy Spirit manifests Himself in prophetic utterance, it is like a light shining on them. Of course, we need to test every prophetic utterance by the word of God, and the witness within our spirit. However, when it is truly of God, it can be like a beacon illuminating the way in which we ought to pray. The unfailing test of whether a prophecy is genuine or not is whether what is uttered is fulfilled.

David Wilkerson's Prophecy

Years ago the Holy Spirit used David Wilkerson to warn the United States that serious trouble and judgment was coming on that nation. That prophetic utterance has not yet been completely fulfilled. The beginning of that fulfilment was 9/11, but there is much more to come. The prophetic utterance the Lord gave him should have been enough, however, to activate and energise prayer warriors in the United States to intercede on behalf of their nation. In a real sense David Wilkerson's prophecy is a light illuminating the way in which we ought to pray for the United States. Certainly it seems that America is on a downhill path, and much more serious judgment is coming. I have myself likened the States to the ship, Titanic, which was thought to be unsinkable but was, in fact, sailing into an iceberg with all lights blazing and the bands playing. It sank within a very short time.

In 1998 David Wilkerson published a book entitled, "God's Plan to Protect His People in the Coming Depression." It was prophetic and began to be fulfilled in 2008. This kind of prophetic utterance or writing is a light on our path that we might understand how to pray and intercede.

The Prophetic Conference in Carmel and Jerusalem, April 1986

There was a conference of Christian leaders on prophecy in April 1986 that was held on Mount Carmel and concluded with a final meeting in Jerusalem. There was a prophetic utterance that the Lord would judge the Soviet Union and the Kremlin for all that it had done. I will only quote a part of it:

"It will not be long before there will come upon the world a time of unparalleled upheaval and turmoil. Do not fear; it is I the Lord who am shaking all things. I began this shaking with the First World War, and I greatly increased it through the Second World War. Since 1973 I have given it an even greater impetus. In the last stage, I plan to complete it with the shaking of the universe itself, with signs in sun and moon and stars. But before that point is reached, I will judge the nations and the time is near. It will not only be by war and civil war, by anarchy and terrorism, and by monetary collapses that I will judge the nations, but also by natural disasters—by earthquake, shortages and famines, and old and new plague diseases. I will also judge them by giving them over to their own ways, to lawlessness, to loveless selfishness, to delusion and to believing a lie, to false religion and an apostate church, even to a Christianity without Me.

Do not fear when these things begin to happen, for I will disclose these things to you before they commence, in order that you might be prepared, and that in the day of trouble and of evil, you may stand firm and overcome. For I purpose that you may become the means of encouraging and strengthening many who love Me but are weak. I desire that through you many may become strong in Me, and that multitudes of others might find My salvation through you.

And hear this! Do not fear the power of the Kremlin nor the power of the Islamic Revolution, for I plan to break both of them through Israel. I will bring down their pride and their arrogance, and shatter them because they have blasphemed My Name. In that day I will avenge the blood of all the martyrs and of innocent ones whom they have slaughtered. I will surely do this thing, for they have thought that there was no one to judge them. But I have seen their ways, and I have heard the cries of the oppressed and the persecuted, and I will break their power and make an end of them. Be therefore prepared, for when all this comes to pass, to you will be given the last great opportunity to preach the gospel freely to all the nations."

This prophetic utterance gave us all much illumination as to the course that contemporary history was taking. It also gave us clear direction as to how to pray for the Soviet Union and its empire, and its many satellites. The Lord would break its enormous power and the grip it had on so many. We were also warned to take seriously the Islamic Revolution and Revival.

A few years before this prophetic utterance, the Soviet Empire was led by a highly influential KGB officer, Yuri Andropov. His influence permeated even the immediate years after he stepped down in 1984, and the Soviet Union seemed as powerful as ever; therefore it appeared unlikely that it would break up, let alone be ended. However, within a few years of that prophetic utterance it had all happened. The Soviet Empire broke up. Many of the Soviet states within it, such as Kazakhstan, Uzbekistan, Azerbaijan, even Georgia and Armenia became free (in fact there are more states than I have mentioned which have also become free). The grip of Marxism on Russia was loosened; the Wall dividing Berlin was destroyed and East and West Germany were reunited; the Iron Curtain fell; and the whole of Eastern Europe and the Baltic States were freed. Many of those states today are part of the European Union.

Incredibly, the old national flag of Russia with its white, red and blue bands replaced the Soviet Union's red flag with its yellow hammer and sickle. No one who has lived through that era of the domination of International Marxism which was centred in the Kremlin could ever have believed that this would happen. Even the double-headed eagle with the crown above the two heads, which represented old Russia under the Czars, appeared on the wall of the cabinet room of the new Russian government. Half the evangelical world believed that Marxism, centred in the Kremlin, was the predicted Anti-Christ which would take the whole world. Yet the Lord smashed it and broke it up.

Even more remarkable, in the nineteen-nineties, the Patriarch of the Russian Orthodox Church was allowed to conduct a solemn service of repentance for the murder of the Czar, the Czarina, and the Czarevich (Crown Prince). It began in the Cathedral and then proceeded in a sombre march around the Kremlin with candles and portraits of the murdered Royal family. Amazingly, the President of Russia, Boris Yeltsin, was present along with other leaders. No one who has lived through this era would have ever believed that this could happen or was even possible! It is astonishing to recognise that seventy years after the Marxist Constitution was signed in the Kremlin Palace it was torn up and discarded in the same Kremlin Palace.

This prophetic utterance was like light shining on what appeared to be an impossibility. For those who were watching, as well as praying, the Lord gave the right weapons to pray for the break-up of the Soviet Marxist Empire, for the releasing and for the upbuilding of the church of God in Russia, in the former Soviet States, and in the erstwhile Communist States of the Baltic and of Eastern Europe. For some Christians it gave a clear understanding of the course that their work should take.

The International Intercessor Leaders Conference—November 1998

Here is another illustration. In one of the biennial International Intercessors leaders' conferences, which was held in Caliraya, Laguna, the Philippines, in November 1998, a prophetic utterance was given. I quote only a portion of that word.

"My anger is stirred up," says the Lord, "against those nations for they are dividing My land and seeking to destroy My heritage. My furious anger is like a boiling cauldron against those powerful states that have produced such strategies and who, by pressure and manipulation, are seeking to implement them. Now I will become their enemy, says the Lord, and I will judge them with natural disasters, by physical catastrophes, by fire, by flood, by earthquake and by eruptions. I will touch the seas, the atmosphere, the earth and all that is within them. Moreover, I will touch them where it will hurt them the most, for I will touch their power and the foundations of their affluence and prosperity. I will smash their prosperous economies, says the Lord. And I will overturn, and overturn, and overturn that they may know that I am the LORD. They sit like potentates, so safe, so secure, believing in their own cleverness and wisdom and power but I, the Lord, will cause them to stumble. I will lead them into confusion and disorder. I will blind them and delude them so that they will make mistakes, because they have not regarded Me nor honoured Me. Instead, they have devalued Me, deriding My word and ignoring My covenants. For too long I have been quiet," says the Lord, "but now will I arise in overflowing anger and fury. In dividing My land and seeking to demoralise and destroy My people Israel, they have thrown down the gauntlet. I, the Lord of Hosts, the Almighty One, will take them on."

When this prophetic utterance came to the intercessor leaders, it was at a time of great economic prosperity, a boom in the housing market, and seeming solid financial stability. To all of us it seemed as if the prophecy was far removed from reality. Nonetheless, in 2008, ten years later, it all began to be fulfilled. Since then it has grown in power, with deep recession, high unemployment, and economic and financial instability. At the same time we have seen earthquakes, tsunamis, volcanic eruptions, floods of what the media has called, "Biblical proportions," terrible fires, and the like.

At least forty-two national intercession movements were represented at this conference, and it gave us all the opportunity to pray for the future of the nations. It also gave some light as to the strategic position and importance which Israel occupies in the purpose and economy of God. It helped us to recognise that we could not hold a balanced and sound eschatological view without understanding Israel. We also understood from this prophetic utterance the danger which the Islamic Revolution and Revival present, and the part Israel will play, by the hand of God, in its destruction.

It would always be good if we were to remember the words that the apostle Paul wrote concerning prophetic utterance: "Do not quench the Spirit; do not despise prophetic utterances. But examine everything carefully; hold fast to that which is good; abstain from every form of evil" (1 Thessalonians 5:19–22 NASB).

The Other Four Gifts

The four gifts—healing, the effecting of miracles, various kinds of tongues, and the interpretation of tongues—may at times have a very important part to play in corporate prayer; although this manifestation of the Spirit may have more to do with other meetings of the people of God. For instance, a tongue and its interpretation in a time of corporate prayer may be a prophetic utterance, or a word of knowledge, or a word of wisdom. The Lord may be emphasing a matter in this more distinctive manner. The gifts of healing and the effecting of miracles may also flow out of a time of corporate prayer.

The Lord Using His Word to Direct Us

Many times the manifestation of the Spirit is expressed by the use of the word of God. In a time of corporate prayer, the Holy Spirit brings to some child of God a scripture which he or she reads out, and it unlocks for all of us the mind and will of the Lord. Such contributions of scripture under the government of the Spirit, may become a word of knowledge, or a word of wisdom, or a word of prophecy, and should be taken up and acted upon by the others in that prayer time. Often it has been my experience that the Lord has used some member of the body to show us the way ahead; at times the Lord has led us into the fulfilment of His will through such contributions. Someone had a word of scripture on their heart, read it, and left others to judge it. When it was taken up by all, we so often came into the fulfilment of His mind and heart. The use of the word of God in corporate prayer is of the highest value.

Prayer Which is Inaudible and Inexpressible

The apostle Paul writes of a ministry of prayer which is inaudible. This ministry of the Holy Spirit in our spirit is deeper than words, deeper than even a tongue, and deeper than utterance. It is an intercession that cannot be expressed in any audible language or manner. The Holy Spirit is interceding in us *for the saints* and it is *according to the will of God*. This ministry of travail is an agonizing of the Holy Spirit in our spirit; it is trapped unexpressed within the child of God and will always have a result.

"And in like manner the Spirit also helpeth our infirmity: for we know not how to pray as we ought; but the Spirit Himself maketh intercession for us with groanings which cannot be uttered; and he that searcheth the hearts knoweth what is the mind of the Spirit, because He maketh in-tercession for the saints according to the will of God" (Romans 8:26–27). This is also a manifestation of the Spirit. The deepest mystery is that the expression in audible and understandable words in prayer is the least part of it! It is like the tip of an iceberg; the majority of it is hidden under the surface. This kind of intercession is in our spirit, and it is the Holy Spirit at work within us.

It is only found in those who are totally devoted to the Lord and committed to Him. Such children of God have a ministry in their spirit, which only the Lord can read, receive and understand. It is an unceasing ministry of intercession. It is a fulfilment of the word: "Pray without ceasing" (1 Thessalonians 5:17).

Corporate Prayer is a Two-Way Exchange

The time of corporate prayer is not only a time when we pour out all our needs, our burdens, and our petitions to the Lord; it is also a time when He speaks to us, revealing His mind and will. The incredible mindset that has developed amongst many Christians is that in a prayer time we have to do all the talking; we do not even expect the Lord to speak to us. Indeed, if the Lord was to answer our earnest and beseeching appeal and speak, many of us would drop dead with shock! We do not expect a corporate time of prayer to be a place where the Lord speaks to us; it is a time only for our speaking to the Lord.

The Lord Jesus went to the heart of the matter when He said: "My sheep hear my voice, and I know them, and they follow me" (John 10:27). In other words, He desires, not only to hear our voice expressing our needs and concerns, but wants us to hear His voice and follow Him. It is noteworthy that He speaks of *following Him.* We need direction from the Lord if we are truly to follow Him and do His will. How many times I have watched and heard the shepherd leading his flock. He talks to them in a language which is neither, Hebrew, Greek, or English, or any other human language, but the sheep understand him. It is the goats which present the problem; they willfully do not hear and disobey the shepherd. They want to follow their own will, their own mind, and their own satisfaction. It is a necessity however to hear the Lord if we will follow Him. There is no alternative to hearing His voice!

Many years ago I was plagued by a sister who always tried to get through to me on the telephone. She lived more than a hundred miles away. At Halford House we all knew that the moment we took up the phone and heard her voice, it would be at least forty-five to fifty minutes; and in that time we would not get a word in edgeways. Therefore, Margaret Trickey, who looked after the house, and others, tried to shield me from her. However, there were times late in the evening when I was working on a Bible study or Bible research relating to the study and was the only person in the place, and the phone would ring and it would be this sister. She always exploded with: "Praise the Lord or hallelujah; at last I have got through to you. God has given you such a gift of counsel and wisdom, and I need to avail myself of it." Before I could even say a word, she started to pour out whatever concern was on her heart.

It was always an overflowing of words. It seemed she hardly took a breath, and I found that it was impossible to say anything—not a single word. All through her speaking, every now and again, she told me how gifted I was with wisdom from the Lord, and then went on expressing her concern. This happened so often that actually I used to put the phone down and carry on with my study or research; now and again just taking it up and saying "yes." After about forty-five or fifty minutes she would say, "Praise the

Lord, you have given me the counsel to do exactly what I thought I should do. Thank you again for being so available to the Lord." And with that she would ring off. I never had the chance to give her any counsel, or express any wisdom that she thought the Lord might have given me. If I had shouted at the top of my voice to her, I do not think she would have heard, because she was so full of the concern that was on her mind.

This is exactly like some of our prayer times. The dear Lord is bombarded with our concerns, with our burdens, and with our petitions, and has no chance whatsoever to utter His voice! There is not even an expectation that He would speak. Yet in the prayer time the Lord is often praised as a wonderful counsellor, and He is told that all the treasures of wisdom and knowledge are hidden in Him and that the Holy Spirit is able to make that wisdom a practical reality to us. If He were to speak, however, as I have already written, many of us in the prayer time would either faint or have a heart attack!

The lesson we need to learn from this illustration is simple and clear. We should expect the Lord to reveal His mind concerning the burdens or petitions that we are making. Corporate prayer is a two-way exchange.

Practical Points

Firstly: Always be available to the Holy Spirit. Many times He is unable to manifest Himself because we are unavailable. Often we think that it is enough that we are there to pray! When we come into a time of corporate prayer, we should bow our head and deliberately make ourselves available for His use in whatever way He chooses. Some Christians get very nervous about the Holy Spirit manifesting Himself, but that is no excuse for our unavailability. It may be that He will put a scripture on your heart that will be a word of knowledge, or a word of wisdom, or even a prophetic utterance giving light on a situation or problem. However, we have to be available to him.

Secondly: Expect the Holy Spirit to prompt you and enable you to contribute. He fully understands your fear of making a mistake, or that you feel you are giving to yourself a greater prominence than you should have. However, let the Holy Spirit decide that! True humility is to be ready for the Lord to speak through you!

Thirdly: Learn from any mistake you make; remember all of us will make mistakes. We learn more from our mistakes as we grow up than in any other way. It is what we do with our mistakes that counts. It is a false humility to go into a deep depression over the mistakes we make and proceed to beat ourselves. In a time of corporate prayer the problem is that everyone knows when we make a mistake and our pride and self-estimate receives a hard blow. If, however, we learn from our mistakes, we grow in the grace and in the knowledge of the Lord.

One remembers the story of a brother who said, "Thus saith the Lord; do not fear My children, for I am with you. As Joshua led the children of Israel through the Red Sea, so will I protect and lead you. Do not fear." Then the brother said, "The Lord saith; I have made a mistake! It was Moses who led them through the Red Sea, not Joshua!" This was a mistake made in front of everyone and obviously was not a manifestation of the Spirit! One hopes that the brother learnt from his mistake!

Fourthly: Be yourself in the Lord. Do not use an artificial or a theatrical voice when the Holy Spirit manifests Himself in you. Use your normal voice and behave in your normal manner. Only remember to speak up so that everyone can hear you. What is the difference between the normal voice you use in prayer and the expression of a gift? Why do we feel that we have to become like Shakespearean actors and actresses when we use a gift? In fact many are disconcerted by such abnormality and become so distracted that they lose the leading of the Holy Spirit. When a person either shouts a gift at the top of their voice, or shrieks a tongue or prophecy, it is more an evidence of the flesh than a manifestation of the Holy Spirit!

Fifthly: Faith is always the basis for the manifestation of the Spirit and not emotion. We need to be careful that we do not exercise a spiritual gift on the basis of emotion or feeling. Some Christians seem to have the idea that the only time you can ever use such a gift is when you are engulfed with a wave of emotion and feeling. The basis for prophetic utterance in the pagan or occult world is always that a spirit possesses you, and suspends your normal judgment. You are not even aware of what you are saying or the actions you are taking. With mediums in the occult everywhere, wizards and witches in Africa and Asia, this is normally the case. When the Holy Spirit manifests Himself through a believer, that believer is always in possession of their normal judgment. They may not understand all that the Lord is saying through them, and may need to enquire of the Lord as to what it means, but their mind is not suspended. Remember the words of the apostle Paul: "The spirits of the prophets are subject to the prophets; for God is not a God of confusion, but of peace" (1 Corinthians 14:32–33).

Sixthly: Spiritual gifts should never be used to manipulate or to impose one's opinion on a time of corporate prayer. That is always the flesh operating. It is interesting in this connection to remember the embargo placed by the Lord on the holy anointing oil touching the flesh (see Exodus 30:31–33). When a child of God consistently abuses corporate prayer, seeking in one way or another to manipulate the time and to impose their opinion on it, the responsible brothers for that time should speak with that person and seek to correct that one.

Lastly: As I have already written, the time of corporate prayer is like a thermometer registering the health, or otherwise, of a fellowship or an assembly. It is in fact the body of the Messiah in action. The apostle Paul writing to the Ephesians said: "We are to grow up in all aspects into him, who is the head, even Christ, from whom the whole body, being fitted and held together by what every joint supplies, according to the proper working of each individual part, causes the growth of the body for the building up of itself in love" (Ephesians 4:15–16 NASB). Please note carefully three matters: "that which every joint supplies; according to the proper working of each individual part; causes the growth of the body for the building up of itself in love." We cannot grow up in all aspects into Him who is the Head, nor can we know the healthy and normal functioning of the body nor the body being fitted and held together, except through that which every joint supplies. Those joints are us, and everything depends on whether we are contributing what we are receiving from the Lord!

The growth of the body and the building up of itself in love is according to the proper working of each individual part. We are the individual parts of the body, and its growth and building up is dependent upon our involvement in it. Corporate prayer is all of this in action.

Other books by Lance Lambert

The Uniqueness of Israel

Woven into the fabric of Jewish existence there is an undeniable uniqueness. There is bitter controversy over the subject of Israel, but time itself will establish the truth about this nation's place in God's plan. For Lance Lambert, the Lord Jesus is the key that unlocks Jewish history He is the key not only to their fall, but also to their restoration. For in spite of the fact that they rejected Him, He has not rejected them.

Jacob I Have Loved

There is no greater example of how God shapes a person than through the story of Jacob. *Jacob I Have Loved* is far more than a biblical overview of the story of Jacob. It is an outstanding illustration of God's desire to utterly transform our fallen inner nature. Despite a twisted, deceiving, and sinful heart, Jacob nonetheless inherited God's richest blessings and became one of the patriarchs of our faith. The amazing truth is that Jacob's name has not been forgotten, as have so many other names in history. Incredibly, it is forever linked with God. His story is an integral part of the history of divine redemption. This book is about the power of God to transform a human life.

Jacob's story is our story.

www.ingramcontent.com/pod-product-compliance
Lightning Source LLC
LaVergne TN
LVHW091138080826
845145LV00008B/2185

* 9 7 8 1 6 8 3 8 9 1 3 6 9 *